super healthy
COOKIES

50 Gluten-Free, Dairy-Free Recipes *for* **Delicious & Nutritious Treats**

BY HALLIE KLECKER

Pure Living Press

MIDDLETON, WISCONSIN

Published in the United States by Pure Living Press, Middleton, Wisconsin.

ISBN 978-0-9858885-0-3
Library of Congress Control Number: 2012915378

Cover and interior design: Alexa Croft, LEKS Creative
Front cover and interior photographs: © Hallie Klecker
Back cover photographs: Cookie © Gabor Kecskemeti /depositphotos.com, Hallie Klecker © Mike Tittel Photography

Disclaimer: This book as been written and produced for informational and educational purposes only. Statements within this book have not been approved by the FDA. Content should not be considered a substitute for professional medical expertise. The reader assumes full responsibility for consulting a qualified health professional before starting a new diet or health program. Please seek professional help regarding any health conditions or concerns. The author and publisher of this book are not responsible for adverse reactions, effects, or consequences resulting from the use of any recipes or suggestions herein or procedures undertaken hereafter.

First Edition

CONTENTS

CHEWY FIG & OAT BARS (Page 68)

DEDICATION

To my dad, a guy with a big
sweet tooth and an even
bigger heart.

Thank you for boosting my
confidence on the down days,
eating my awful cookie disasters,
and loving me through the
thick and the thin.

It means more than you know.

GROWN-UP MONSTER COOKIES (Page 91)

INTRODUCTION

Moist, chewy, crispy, crunchy, ooey, gooey, buttery, nutty . . . who doesn't love cookies in their many mouthwatering forms?

I was born a cookie monster. In one of my earliest memories, my mom and I are huddled in the kitchen baking up a batch of chocolate chip cookies and eating way too much dough in the process. Trips to my grandma's house always involved raiding the freezer for handfuls of her soft peanut butter cookies and chocolate walnut drops. As I got older and began more experimentation of my own in the kitchen, I would make cookies and other confections around the holidays as though it were a part time job. I read cookie cookbooks before I went to bed at night just for fun. See the theme here? I think it's safe to say that I've been cookie obsessed from the get-go.

In my late teens, I began experiencing a slew of health issues that led me to discover my food sensitivities to gluten and dairy. Eliminating them from my diet was the best thing I've ever done for my health. I put my love for baking on hold for a while, unsure how I would go about making my beloved cookies without wheat flour or butter.

Over the years as I fortified my diet with whole and natural foods, I began to timidly dip my toe in the world of gluten-free baking. Countless cookie catastrophes fell like roadblocks in my path, but they didn't stop me. I was determined to make healthy treats that still tasted fabulous.

After writing my blog, Daily Bites (www.DailyBitesBlog.com), for several years, I took a big leap in 2011 and published my first cookbook, *The Pure Kitchen*. The baked goods and desserts in that book were so much fun for me to create and received such a positive response from readers that I decided my next book would be entirely devoted to healthy sweets. And what better topic than super healthy cookies?

What makes these cookies super healthy? For starters, everything in this book is 100% gluten-free, dairy-free, and refined sugar-free. Using whole grain gluten-free flours and limited starches along with nut and seed flours, these treats are higher in fiber, vitamins and minerals, and protein than your average cookies. Natural sweeteners like honey, coconut sugar, and dates take the place of bleached granulated cane sugar for a healthier approach that will still have your taste buds singing. Unlike most gluten-free baked good recipes, these cookies don't require any gums or strange binders to hold them together. When a little extra binding power is needed, I use high-fiber flaxseed, chia seeds, and psyllium husks.

I serve these cookies to a wide variety of people, many of them having little or no desire to eat healthier or gluten-free. They still love these cookies. Many of the recipes are so healthy you can even eat them for breakfast without an ounce of guilt. (I'm giving you permission to do this. You're welcome!)

Each recipe in this book has been given a sweetness rating indicating its level of sweetness as low, medium, or high. You'll see a sweetness key in the sidebar of each recipe with three spoons, like these:

SWEETNESS RATING
LOW   MEDIUM   HIGH

One shaded spoon equals a low sweetness level, two shaded spoons equal medium sweetness, and three shaded spoons equal highly sweet. I often serve low-sweetness cookies for breakfast or brunch, while I reserve high-sweetness treats for special occasions or when I'm battling a particularly pesky sweet tooth.

Please bear in mind that because these recipes are naturally sweetened, they may not taste as sweet as cookies found in the common household cookie jar. Be okay with that and know that over time, as you eat less refined sugar and more natural sweeteners, your taste buds will adapt. I was amazed to find that after eating refined sugar-free for a few months, naturally sweetened goodies tasted incredibly indulgent to my palate.

Something about homemade cookies just brings a smile to my face. And the fact that you can now enjoy sweet treats with a much healthier spin makes me all the more delighted. Like all food, these cookies taste best when savored in the company of those you love. So share them with your family, friends, neighbors, coworkers, and anyone else who needs a little drop of joy in their lives.

Enjoy and happy baking!

The Virtual Bakery

For a photo collection of over half of the recipes in this book, visit:
www.DailyBitesBlog.com/CookbookGallery

Super Healthy Cookies
101

INGREDIENTS

The majority of the ingredients used in these recipes are easy to find at natural food stores, co-ops, and even large supermarkets. Check out the Resources section (page 121) for details on recommended gluten-free brands.

Grains & Flours

Almond flour, blanched: Made from finely ground blanched almonds, this high-protein, low-carbohydrate flour lends a lovely crumb to baked goods and does not taste gritty. Note that almond flour is often labeled "almond meal." Store it in the refrigerator or freezer. Bring to room temperature before measuring.

Arrowroot starch: Also called arrowroot powder or arrowroot flour, this ingredient is made from the ground roots of the arrowroot plant. It gives gluten-free baked goods a light texture and sturdy structure without imparting a strong flavor. Store at room temperature.

Brown rice flour: I use brown rice flour in conjunction with other flours, grains, or nuts as it often lends a gritty texture to the final product if used exclusively. Store at room temperature or in the freezer for longterm storage.

Buckwheat flour: Perhaps my favorite gluten-free flour, recipes made with buckwheat flour pack hearty, earthy flavor into every bite. Contrary to what many people think, buckwheat actually contains no wheat at all. It comes from a seed related to rhubarb. Store buckwheat flour in the refrigerator or freezer. Bring to room temperature before measuring.

Coconut flour: High-protein, high-fiber coconut flour is like a sponge, absorbing incredible amounts of liquid! If you don't like the flavor of coconut, don't worry. This flour is fairly mild and does not lend a strong coconut flavor to most baked goods. Store it in the refrigerator or freezer. Bring to room temperature before measuring.

Gluten-free rolled oats: Be sure to buy certified gluten-free oats, as most "regular" oats are manufactured in a plant that processes wheat, causing high risk for cross-contamination. Old fashioned oats are a good source of fiber and supply trace minerals such as manganese and selenium. Store at room temperature.

Quinoa flakes: Essentially just steamrolled quinoa, quinoa flakes make a wonderful addition to gluten-free baked goods. High in protein and fiber, they add texture and subtle grassy flavor while packing in stellar nutrition, too. Store quinoa flakes at room temperature.

Sweeteners

Applesauce, unsweetened: Adding unsweetened applesauce to recipes contributes subtle sweetness as well as moisture. When whisked with ground chia seeds or flaxseeds, it can also help bind gluten-free baked goods together and keep them from crumbling.

Blackstrap molasses: When cane sugar is refined, the leftover product is molasses. Packed with iron and other minerals, molasses contributes a robust flavor to baked goods even when used in small amounts. Choose molasses labeled "unsulphured," as this means that no sulphur was used during the extraction process.

Coconut sugar: Also known as palm sugar, this unrefined granulated sweetener is rich in vitamins and minerals, making it a smart alternative to bleached cane sugar. Coconut sugar is made from the sap of palm tree blossoms and lends subtle molasses notes to baked goods.

Grade B maple syrup: Full-bodied and flavorful, maple syrup contains minerals including zinc and manganese. Grade B is the darkest and least refined variety of maple syrup, so it is the preferable choice, although Grade A will work in a pinch.

Honey: Pure honeys vary widely in flavor, color, and consistency depending on the source of the nectar that the bees collected, making it a truly artisanal ingredient. Experiment with different varieties (alfalfa, clover, wildflower, and more) to find your favorite. I often use local, organic clover honey in my baking for its mild flavor.

Fats & Oils

Coconut oil, virgin: The most common oil I use in cookies and baked goods is unrefined, virgin, organic coconut oil. It is a nutrient-packed saturated fat that many consider to be antibacterial, antimicrobial, and helpful in metabolism regulation. I find the flavor of coconut oil to be fairly neutral in baked goods, although it may taste nutty or "tropical" to some palates. It works wonders as a naturally dairy-free substitute for butter.

Olive oil, extra-virgin: A staple of the Mediterranean diet, extra-virgin olive oil is made from the first cold press of olives and is rich in heart-healthy fats. When used in baked goods in small amounts, it adds moisture and promotes a smooth mouthfeel. Purchase olive oil in dark glass bottles and store in a cool, dark place for no more than a few months.

Nut butters: Almond, peanut, and sunflower seed butter add richness to many of my cookie recipes. They also help hold certain cookies together and keep them moist.

Nuts & seeds: Not only do nuts and seeds contribute flavor and texture to cookies, but they also can be ground into meals and used as a flour-like base for the recipe. When toasted, they take on entirely new flavor profiles and add incredible dimension.

Binders

Ground flaxseed & chia seeds: Because gluten-free cookies lack the structure and elasticity that the gluten in wheat flour provides, it is often necessary to add a binder that will help hold the cookie together. Instead of using gums (such as xanthan or guar gum), I prefer to use ground flaxseeds and chia seeds for their natural binding power. They are also excellent sources of fiber and essential fatty acids. You can purchase the seeds whole and grind them yourself in a coffee grinder. Store the ground seeds in the refrigerator or freezer.

Whole psyllium husks: Although commonly used as a fiber supplement, whole psyllium husks also help give dough some elasticity when used in small amounts. The whole husks dissolve into the dough and are not detectable in taste or texture. Find them at health food stores, co-ops, and pharmacies.

Other Ingredients

Citrus zest: Adding finely grated citrus zest to certain cookies enhances their fruity qualities while also incorporating antioxidants and essential oils.

Ground cinnamon: What would a baking book be without the mother of all spices? An ingredient with ancient roots, cinnamon was imported to Egypt as early as 2000 BC. Organic cinnamon finds its way into many of my cookie recipes for both its flavor and nutritive properties.

Sea salt: I use finely ground sea salt in all of my recipes and highly recommend it. Store it at room temperature in a cool, dark place. It will last indefinitely. I keep a little silver bowl of sea salt on my counter at all times for convenience when I'm cooking and baking.

Unsweetened chocolate & cocoa powder: Because dark chocolate contains cane sugar, I prefer to use organic unsweetened chocolate and cocoa powder in conjunction with natural sweeteners to yield a similar result in healthier way.

Vanilla extract: It is generally accepted that vanilla extract is gluten-free. It comes in both alcohol and non-alcoholic varieties. Experiment with different vanilla extracts to find the one you like best, choosing organic if possible. Note that alcohol-based extracts may impart a "boozy" flavor to some recipes if used in excess or if unbaked.

CHUNKY MONKEY COOKIES (Page 26)

Investing in good quality equipment and tools will produce superior results in the world of baking. Here's what you'll need to make the cookies in this book:

Baking sheets: Use rimmed baking sheets made of heavy stainless steel so they don't warp in the heat of the oven.

Cutting boards: My large wooden cutting board gets the most use of any of my kitchen tools. Not only do I use it for chopping, but it also makes a great surface for rolling dough and shaping cookies.

Digital kitchen scale: Using a scale to weigh your gluten-free flours will result in the most accurate results. Purchase a scale that measures in both ounces and grams.

Electric mixer: My stand mixer makes whipping up batters a breeze. An electric handheld mixer will work just as well, though.

Food processor: This tool is essential in the super healthy kitchen! As you make recipes from this book, you'll find yourself using it time and again for everything from chopping nuts to making dough.

Knives: Choose sharp, heavy knives that sit comfortably in your hand. A good quality knife makes all the difference when you're chopping and prepping ingredients.

Measuring cups & spoons: Every baker needs several sets of measuring utensils. I use stainless steel and glass utensils so that hot liquids don't melt the plastic.

Microplane® graters: These handheld graters are essential for grating citrus zest, nutmeg, fresh ginger, chocolate, and more. They are inexpensive and hold their sharpness for a long time.

Mixing bowls: Stocking an assortment of stainless and glass mixing bowls in your kitchen gives you the freedom to make several recipes at once without having to wash bowls all of the time.

Mini muffin pan: A few of the recipes in this book call for a mini muffin pan to make bite-sized treats.

Parchment paper: Lining your baking sheets and pans with parchment paper eliminates the need for cooking spray and prolongs the life of your equipment. If it's not too soiled, you can reuse it, too. Use unbleached parchment paper, which is available at many natural foods stores and online.

Ruler: Keep a ruler in your utensil drawer and reach for it when a recipe calls for a specific measurement (such as the thickness or diameter of dough).

Skillets, pots & pans: Stainless steel cookware cleans up beautifully and lasts for decades. It's all I use.

Spatulas: Keep a thin metal spatula around for working with delicate cookies. A few rubber spatulas are also essential for mixing and handling dough.

Whisks & spoons: Every good cook needs their share of whisks, wooden spoons, and the all important tasting spoons, too.

Before You Bake

Please, please, please read the recipe all the way through before starting! Preparation paves the way to success. By reading the entire recipe before tying on that apron and jumping in, you'll know what to expect and can be better prepared and equipped.

I'm all for you tweaking these recipes to your tastes, but I advise that you follow them as written before making changes to them.

Measuring Flour

I created all of the recipes in this book using the "spoon and level" method, so I suggest you use this method as well for the best results. Here's how: stir up the flour in the container or bag before measuring. This incorporates air, often leading to lighter baked goods. Scoop the flour into the measuring cup using a spoon. Use a flat edge, such as a butter knife, to level the flour flush with the top of the cup. Do not pack the flour into the cup or use rounded cups. You will have more flour than you need, leading to various problems that may arise during baking.

Sticky Situation

To prevent sweeteners like maple syrup and honey from sticky to your measuring cups and spoons, lightly oil them with olive oil before measuring. Those sticky sweeteners will slide right out of the cup without the least bit of hassle.

Working with Coconut Oil

Because all of the recipes in this book are dairy-free, I often use virgin coconut oil to replace butter. You'll want to store your coconut oil at room temperature in a cupboard or pantry. When a recipe calls for coconut oil at room temperature, this means that the oil is soft and spreadable but not melted. Coconut oil will retain a soft texture between about 65–78°F. If your kitchen is warmer than 78°F and your oil is beginning to melt, simply measure out what you need and place it in the refrigerator for a few minutes to firm up.

An Egg-cellent Idea

Some of the recipes in this book call for room temperature eggs. If, like me, you don't have all day to sit around waiting for cold eggs to warm up, simply place the egg in a bowl and cover it with warm water. Let it sit for 10–15 minutes and voila! Room temperature egg in a quarter of the time.

In Praise of Parchment

Parchment paper is a baker's best friend. Not only does it make clean up a breeze, but it also saves you the hassle of scraping stubborn cookies off of the baking sheet, therefore prolonging the life of your pans. Some of the bar recipes in this book direct you to line an 8x8-inch baking dish with parchment paper. Here's how:

> Place your dish upside down on a flat surface. Cut a piece of parchment paper that is 2–3 inches larger than your dish on all sides. Center the paper over the inverted dish and press it to the pan, using your hands to mold the paper to the shape of dish. Crease the paper in the corners to help reinforce the shape.

> Remove the paper and turn the dish right side up. Place the molded piece of paper into the dish, making sure there is a slight overhang of paper extending over the edges. (You'll grab this overhang to remove the bars after they've baked.)

Oven Lovin'

Because every oven is different, I recommend that you purchase an inexpensive but accurate oven thermometer (available at most home and kitchen stores) to calibrate your oven. If your oven registers at 350°F when set at 375°F, then you'll know that it runs 25°F low and you can adjust the temperature accordingly when making these recipes.

Let's do a little vocabulary lesson here. Just what exactly does "preheating" mean? As soon as the oven bell rings or the light goes on indicating that it's preheated, we're good to go, right? Not quite. I recommend waiting until your oven has been on for 10–15 minutes past the initial preheating so that it's good and hot before baking.

Unless otherwise noted, rotate your pans halfway through the baking time to ensure even browning. Even the highest quality ovens can have "hot spots." Rotate the pans from front to back so that the cookies that were closer to the back of the oven face the front when rotated. If you have two pans in the oven, rotate them from top to bottom as well.

Doubling Recipes

If you would like to make more cookies than the amount indicated in the recipe, make another batch instead of doubling the recipe. I know…I can already hear your moaning! I understand that this requires a bit more effort, but gluten- and dairy-free baking can be kind of funky. I've had the best results making multiple batches instead of one huge batch.

That Virtue Called Patience

As tempting as it can be to snag a cookie from the baking sheet when it's still warm from the oven, do yourself a big favor and wait until the cookies are cooled completely to try them. Many of the cookies in this book firm up and "bond" as they cool on the baking sheets, so it's very important not to rush that process. If you must take a bite when they're still warm, at least try to wait for 10–15 minutes. Any less than that and your cookie may crumble apart in your hand.

Properly Storing Cookies

Unless otherwise noted, the cookies in this book store well in an airtight container at room temperature for 2–3 days. Any longer than that and you will need to freeze them. (See below.) If you live in a particularly humid climate, consider refrigerating or freezing your cookies immediately after they've cooled.

Properly Freezing Cookies

All of the cookies in this book can be frozen successfully. Here's how to do it: place the cookies in an even layer on a parchment-lined baking sheet or large pan. Freeze, uncovered, until solid. (If your baking sheet won't fit in your freezer, just divide the cookies among smaller pans.) Place the frozen cookies in an airtight container and store for 3–4 weeks.

When it comes to gluten-free baking, you may feel like your questions are as plentiful as stars in the night sky. That's okay! You'll learn more quickly by asking questions and seeking answers. Below are a few frequently asked questions about recipes in this book.

These cookies are so healthy! That means I can eat them by the handfuls, right?

Oh, how I wish the answer to this question was a resounding YES! But remember, our bodies do best when we consume all things with balance in mind. Although these cookies are healthier than most, that doesn't give you a free pass to eat the entire batch on a rainy afternoon. Treats, no matter how healthy, are still just that: treats! Enjoy them in moderation.

Will these cookies taste as sweet as what I'm used to?

If you're used to sugary cookies rich in butter, cane sugar, and refined wheat flour, then no. These cookies will not taste the same. You simply cannot expect a treat made with buckwheat flour, coconut oil, and maple syrup to taste the same as your grandmother's prizewinning cookies. Learn to appreciate the flavors and textures of these recipes for what they are instead of comparing them to what you think they should be.

In my baking, I use natural sweeteners in place of refined sugar and typically use less than most traditional recipes to lend subtle "background sweetness." This allows the other flavors in the recipe to shine through. Training your taste buds to respond positively to less sweet baked goods will take time, but before you know it you'll be shocked at how sweet something like a banana can taste after you've been avoiding refined sugar for a while.

What can I substitute for eggs in these recipes?

There are many naturally egg-free recipes in this book. For those that contain eggs, I spent a great deal of time developing them as they're written and have found that the eggs are very important to the structure of the recipe. If you'd like to try substituting a chia or flaxseed slurry for an egg, feel free. But please know that I cannot guarantee successful results. (To make a chia or flaxseed slurry, whisk 1 tablespoon of ground seed with 3 tablespoons of water. Set aside to thicken for 5 minutes.)

I don't have a natural food store nearby and can't find many of the ingredients used in these recipes. What should I do?

Shop online! Thank heavens for Amazon.com. You can purchase virtually every single ingredient used in these recipes on the web, often getting great deals in the process.

How should I store and freeze my cookies?

See the tips on page 16 for storing and freezing instructions. Always store cookies in an airtight container such as a sealable food storage bag or hard-sided container with a tight-fitting lid.

I'm overwhelmed. Where should I start?

If you're new to healthy gluten-free baking, welcome! My advice is to start slow and steady with some of the more familiar ingredients. Good beginner recipes in this book are the Chewy Cashew Apricot Cookies on page 108, the Blueberry Gingerbread Cookie Dough Balls on page 71, and the Bear Paw Freezer Treats on page 44.

Remember that all baking, including gluten-free baking, is supposed to be fun and relaxing! View it as a learning experience instead of a stress inducer. A positive attitude will take you a long way.

CHERRY ALMOND BREAKFAST BISCUITS (Page 23)

FRUITY
COOKIES

Fruit is nature's perfect sweetener. In this section, you'll find a handful of mouthwatering cookies that get a natural boost of sweetness from fresh, dried, and preserved fruit. Because they're packed with wholesome ingredients, don't feel the least bit guilty about sneaking a cookie (or two or three) for breakfast. Not that I've ever done that before...

HEALING
BITES

Three Cheers for Carrots

Carrots contain beta-carotene, an antioxidant compound that the body converts to vitamin A. Essential for healthy skin and eyes, vitamin A also helps boost the immune system and nourish the body's cells and tissues. When added to baked goods, grated carrots contribute moisture, texture, and subtle sweetness that pairs well with bananas and applesauce. Carrots have a very long shelf life when stored in the refrigerator, so I always keep them on hand.

Bunny Bites

These bite-sized cookies remind me of carrot cake. Maple syrup adds the perfect layer of earthy sweetness, while carrots, walnuts, oats, and shredded coconut lend hearty texture. A few of these cookies with a green smoothie makes for a fabulous breakfast!

MAKES
About 24
chewy cookies

**SWEETNESS
RATING**

INGREDIENTS

2/3 cup raw walnuts, finely chopped

1/2 cup (67 grams) brown rice flour

1/2 cup gluten-free rolled oats

1/2 cup unsweetened shredded coconut

3 tablespoons ground flaxseed

2 teaspoons ground cinnamon

1/2 teaspoon baking powder

1/4 teaspoon sea salt

1 cup (loosely packed) coarsely grated carrots (about 2 medium carrots, grated)

1 medium ripe banana, mashed well (about 1/3–1/2 cup mashed)

1/4 cup Grade B maple syrup

2 tablespoons extra-virgin olive oil or melted coconut oil

DIRECTIONS

Preheat the oven to 350°F. Line a baking sheet with parchment paper.

In a large bowl, whisk together the walnuts, brown rice flour, oats, coconut, flaxseed, cinnamon, baking powder, and salt. In a separate bowl, whisk together the carrots, mashed banana, maple syrup, and oil. Stir the carrot mixture into the dry ingredients until a thick dough forms.

Roll the dough into 1-inch balls. Flatten the balls between your palms to form small cookies about 1/3–inch thick. Place the cookies 1 inch apart on the baking sheet.

Bake for about 15 minutes or until golden brown and firm to the touch. Cool completely. Store in an airtight container in the refrigerator.

WELLNESS
TIP

Smart Start

Get a smart start to your day. Incorporate almonds and almond flour into breakfast treats for a boost of plant-based protein and healthy fats that will keep you going strong all day long. Nutrient-dense almonds will keep hunger at bay and help you stay satisfied.

Cherry Almond Breakfast Biscuits

Growing up in Wisconsin, my family and I took many a summer vacation to Door County, an area in the northeastern part of the state known for its quaint cottages, funky art galleries, and sweet cherry orchards. We always came home from our trips with cherry-laden cardboard boxes bouncing around in the backseat, tempting my sister and me to nibble on the fruits all the way home. Paired with almonds and plenty of other wholesome ingredients in these cluster-like biscuits, the dried cherries bring back many sweet memories of those sun-drenched summer days.

MAKES
About 12 biscuits

SWEETNESS RATING

INGREDIENTS

1 cup gluten-free rolled oats
½ cup (48 grams) blanched almond flour
½ cup unsweetened shredded coconut
½ cup dried cherries
⅓ cup raw almonds, chopped
2 tablespoons ground flaxseed
1 teaspoon ground cinnamon
½ teaspoon sea salt
1 medium ripe banana, mashed well (about ⅓–½ cup mashed)
2 tablespoons unsweetened applesauce
2 tablespoons extra-virgin olive oil
1 tablespoon Grade B maple syrup or honey

DIRECTIONS

Preheat the oven to 350°F. Line a baking sheet with parchment paper.

In a large bowl, combine the oats, almond flour, shredded coconut, cherries, almonds, flaxseed, cinnamon, and salt. In a small bowl, whisk together the mashed banana, applesauce, olive oil, and maple syrup. Pour the wet ingredients into the dry and stir to combine.

Form the mixture into tightly-packed biscuit shapes about ½–¾ inch thick, using about 2 tablespoons of dough per biscuit. Place them on the lined baking sheet. Bake for 18–20 minutes until lightly browned. Cool completely. Store in an airtight container.

INGREDIENT
SPOTLIGHT

Maple Syrup

Rich and smooth with deep caramel undertones, Grade B maple syrup is the perfect sweetener to pair with hearty oats and other whole grains. Choosing Grade B maple syrup ensures that you're getting the most nutritious and least refined variety. In addition to adding mouthwatering sweetness to cookies and baked goods, maple syrup lends itself well to many uses in the kitchen:

Add it to green smoothies for a little extra sweetness.

Drizzle it over oatmeal or hot cereal as a healthful alternative to brown sugar.

Mix a tablespoon or two with ground turkey or chicken when making patties for the flavor of breakfast sausage.

Whisk a splash of syrup with oil, vinegar, and Dijon mustard for a quick vinaigrette that's delicious over steamed green beans, broccoli, and more.

Maple Oatmeal Raisin Cookies

I love a chewy cookie, but these thin and crispy oatmeal cookies win me over every time. Their toasty oat flavor pairs perfectly with the natural sweetness of the maple syrup and raisins, just begging to be served with a warm cup of tea.

MAKES
About 20
thin and crispy cookies

SWEETNESS RATING

TECHNIQUE TIP
If you keep your maple syrup in the refrigerator, bring it to room temperature before beating it into coconut oil. Cold maple syrup will cause the oil to harden.

INGREDIENTS

1 ½ cups gluten-free rolled oats, divided use

¼ cup plus 2 tablespoons (51 grams) brown rice flour

¼ cup (27 grams) arrowroot starch

1 tablespoon ground flaxseed

2 teaspoons ground cinnamon

1 teaspoon baking soda

½ teaspoon baking powder

¼ teaspoon sea salt

⅔ cup Grade B maple syrup

¼ cup virgin coconut oil, room temperature (not melted)

½ cup raisins

DIRECTIONS

Preheat the oven to 350°F. Line 2 baking sheets with parchment paper.

In a food processor fitted with the steel blade, grind ½ cup of the oats to form a coarse flour, about 30 seconds. Transfer the oat flour to a large mixing bowl and stir in the remaining 1 cup oats, brown rice flour, arrowroot starch, flaxseed, cinnamon, baking soda, baking powder, and salt.

With an electric mixer on medium speed, beat together the maple syrup and coconut oil until combined. Add the half of the flour mixture and beat to combine. Then beat in the remaining flour mixture. Stir in the raisins by hand.

Drop heaping tablespoons of the dough 2 inches apart onto the lined baking sheets. Use your fingertips to flatten each dough mound slightly to about ½-inch thick.

Bake for 10–12 minutes until golden brown. Cool completely. Store in an airtight container.

Chunky Monkey Cookies

These are the cookies I make when I want banana bread in less than 30 minutes. I love their moist and cake-like texture. If you don't have cacao nibs on hand, simply omit them or swap in dark chocolate chips or raisins.

MAKES
About 18
moist cookies

SWEETNESS RATING

INGREDIENTS

2 medium bananas, mashed well (about 2/3 cup mashed)

¼ cup creamy raw almond butter (unsweetened)

2 tablespoons Grade B maple syrup

2 tablespoons ground flaxseed

1 teaspoon vanilla extract

2/3 cup unsweetened shredded coconut

½ cup (67 grams) brown rice flour

½ raw walnuts, pecans, or macadamia nuts, finely chopped

1 teaspoon baking soda

¼ teaspoon sea salt

¼ cup cacao nibs

DIRECTIONS

Preheat the oven to 350°F. Line 2 baking sheets with parchment paper.

In a medium bowl, whisk together the mashed bananas, almond butter, maple syrup, flaxseed, and vanilla to combine. In a large bowl, combine the shredded coconut, brown rice flour, walnuts, baking soda, and salt. Stir in the banana mixture to combine. Stir in the cacao nibs.

Drop heaping tablespoons of the dough onto the lined baking sheets. Use your fingertips to flatten each cookie to about ½-inch thick. Bake for about 12 minutes or until golden brown. Cool completely. Store in an airtight container.

Apricot Quinoa Cookies

Soft on the inside and slightly crunchy on the outside, these lightly sweetened cookies remind me of muffin tops. The longer they are stored, the softer the cookies become. Quinoa flakes add texture and a subtle grassy flavor that gives them a unique spin. If you don't have dried apricots on hand, swap in raisins, currants, or dried blueberries for equally delicious results.

MAKES
About 15
moist cookies

SWEETNESS RATING

INGREDIENT TIP
When you buy dried apricots, they should be brown, which indicates that they are unsulphured and natural. Bright orange dried apricots have been treated with sulphur dioxide to keep them lighter in color.

INGREDIENTS
½ cup unsweetened applesauce
¼ cup extra-virgin olive oil
¼ cup coconut sugar
3 tablespoons ground flaxseed
1 tablespoon apple cider vinegar
2 teaspoons vanilla extract
1 teaspoon ground cinnamon
¼ teaspoon sea salt
1 cup (96 grams) blanched almond flour
1 cup quinoa flakes
1 teaspoon baking soda
½ cup unsulphured dried apricots, chopped

DIRECTIONS
Preheat the oven to 350°F. Line a baking sheet with parchment paper.

In a large bowl, beat together the applesauce, olive oil, coconut sugar, flaxseed, vinegar, vanilla, cinnamon, and salt with an electric mixer until combined. Add the almond flour, quinoa flakes, and baking soda. Beat to combine. Stir in the dried apricots by hand.

Let the dough stand for 5–10 minutes. Drop heaping tablespoons of the dough 1–2 inches apart onto the lined baking sheet. Gently flatten the cookies to about ⅓-inch thick with your fingertips.

Bake for 18-20 minutes until deeply golden brown and firm to the touch. Cool completely. Store in an airtight container.

INGREDIENT
SPOTLIGHT

Prunes

Long heralded for their high fiber content, prunes (dried plums) also boast an array of disease-fighting antioxidants. Because they're packed with soluble fiber, which may increase insulin sensitivity, prunes can also play a role in preventing type 2 diabetes. The insoluble fiber in prunes promotes optimal intestinal health by feeding good bacteria in the colon.

Grain-Free Granola Cookies

Moist and chewy, these treats taste like a fruity granola bar in cookie form. I call them "snacking cookies" for this very reason. Their sturdy texture makes them a convenient treat to tote along on picnics and hikes, too.

MAKES
About 16
chewy cookies

SWEETNESS RATING

INGREDIENTS
½ cup (packed) pitted Medjool dates
½ cup (packed) pitted dried prunes
3 tablespoons unsweetened applesauce
1 cup raw walnuts, finely chopped
½ cup unsweetened shredded coconut
½ cup raw sunflower seeds
¼ cup raw sesame seeds
2 tablespoons ground flaxseed
2 teaspoons ground cinnamon
¼ teaspoon sea salt
⅓ cup raisins or dried currants

DIRECTIONS
Preheat the oven to 350°F. Line 2 baking sheets with parchment paper.

Place the dates and prunes in a bowl and cover with hot water. Soak for 10 minutes. Drain well and place them in the bowl of a food processor fitted with the steel blade. Add the applesauce and process to form a thick paste with very few chunks, stopping several times to scrape down the sides of the bowl with a rubber spatula.

In a large bowl, combine the walnuts, coconut, sunflower seeds, sesame seeds, flaxseed, cinnamon, and salt. Add the date paste and stir to thoroughly combine. Stir in the raisins.

Form the dough into cookie-shaped patties about ⅓-inch thick and 2½-inches in diameter. Place the cookies on the baking sheets. Bake for about 16 minutes until golden brown. Cool completely. Store in an airtight container.

Banana Raisin Walnut Cookies

A not-too-sweet treat, these flourless cookies are entirely fruit-sweetened, making them an energizing and super healthy snack. The riper your bananas, the sweeter the cookies will turn out. For this recipe I like to use bananas that are very, very speckled with brown spots, almost to the point of being more brown than yellow.

MAKES
About 20
super-moist cookies

SWEETNESS RATING

TECHNIQUE TIP
Because of the ripe bananas, these cookies may stick to the parchment paper as they cool. Use a thin metal spatula to remove them from the pan.

INGREDIENTS
1 ¾ cups raw walnuts, divided use
2 medium very ripe bananas, broken into chunks
¼ cup unsweetened shredded coconut
1 tablespoon ground chia seeds
2 teaspoons ground cinnamon
½ teaspoon baking soda
¼ teaspoon sea salt
½ cup raisins

DIRECTIONS
Preheat the oven to 350°F. Line 2 baking sheets with parchment paper.

Place 1 ½ cups of the walnuts in a food processor fitted with the steel blade. Process until mealy, about 30 seconds. Add the bananas, coconut, ground chia seeds, cinnamon, baking soda, and salt. Process to form a thick batter. Transfer the batter to a mixing bowl.

Chop the remaining ¼ cup of walnuts. Stir them into the cookie batter along with the raisins. Drop tablespoons of the batter 2 inches apart onto the lined baking sheets. Using moist fingertips, flatten each cookie mound to about ⅓-inch thick.

Bake for 10–12 minutes until lightly browned. Cool completely. Store the cookies in an airtight container in the refrigerator.

Almond Butter & Jelly Cookies

Everyone loves a peanut butter and jelly sandwich. This healthful twist on the classic lunchtime staple replaces the peanut butter with creamy roasted almond butter. Each craggily-edged cookie holds a spoonful of sweet fruit jam in the center. These treats are sure to delight cookie-lovers both young and old!

MAKES
About 22
chewy cookies

SWEETNESS RATING

SWAP IT
If you don't have buckwheat flour on hand, replace it with brown rice flour.

INGREDIENTS
1 cup creamy roasted almond butter (unsweetened),
    at room temperature
½ cup coconut sugar
1 large egg
¼ cup (30 grams) buckwheat flour
1 teaspoon baking soda
3-4 tablespoons fruit jam, preferably fruit juice-sweetened

DIRECTIONS
Preheat the oven to 350°F. Line 2 baking sheets with parchment paper.

With an electric mixer on medium speed, beat together the almond butter, coconut sugar, egg, buckwheat flour, and baking soda until a thick dough forms. Roll tablespoons of the dough into balls. It's okay if the dough is oily in your hands. Place the balls 2 inches apart on the lined baking sheets.

Using your knuckle or index finger, make a small indentation (about ¼-inch deep) into the center of each cookie. Some cracks around the edges of the cookies are okay, but pinch any large splits back together gently. Fill the indentations with about ¼-teaspoon of jam.

Bake for 12 minutes. Cool completely. (The cookies will firm up as they cool.) Store in an airtight container.

INGREDIENT
SPOTLIGHT

Blueberries

If you want to optimize your health with just one food, let it be blueberries! Studied for decades for their potent health benefits, blueberries have rightly earned their place in the pantheon of "super foods." Blueberries contain both anthocyanins and flavonols, two phytonutrients that serve a purpose as both antioxidants and anti-inflammatory compounds in the body. A low-glycemic fruit, blueberries are a smart choice for diabetics and those with hypoglycemia as well.

Blueberry Bliss Cookies

Love blueberry muffins? You'll adore these melt-in-your-mouth, tender cookies that just so happen to be grain-free. With a hint of lemon zest and plenty of juicy blueberries speckling the dough, these cookies are the perfect treat to savor all spring and summer long.

MAKES
About 18
moist and tender cookies

SWEETNESS RATING

VARIATION
For a tasty Strawberry Orange cookie, replace the lemon zest with orange zest. Then swap in chopped fresh strawberries for the blueberries.

INGREDIENTS
1 cup (96 grams) blanched almond flour
⅓ cup (39 grams) plus 1 teaspoon (3 grams) coconut flour, divided use
2 tablespoons whole psyllium husks
½ teaspoon baking powder
½ teaspoon baking soda
¼ teaspoon sea salt
½ cup virgin coconut oil, room temperature (not melted)
⅔ cup coconut sugar
1 large egg, room temperature
1 tablespoon finely grated lemon zest
1 teaspoon vanilla extract
½ cup frozen blueberries (not thawed)

DIRECTIONS
Preheat the oven to 350°F. Line 2 baking sheets with parchment paper.

In a medium bowl, whisk together the almond flour, ⅓ cup coconut flour, psyllium husks, baking powder, baking soda, and salt.

With an electric mixer on medium speed, beat together the coconut oil and coconut sugar until creamy, about 1 minute. Add the egg, lemon zest, and vanilla. Beat to combine. Add half of the flour mixture and beat to combine. Then beat in the remaining flour mixture.

In a small bowl, toss the frozen blueberries with the remaining 1 teaspoon coconut flour. Stir the blueberries into the dough by hand just to combine. Try to avoid breaking the berries. Drop heaping tablespoons of the dough 2 inches apart onto the lined baking sheets. Flatten each cookie mound to about ½-inch thick with your fingertips.

Bake for about 12 minutes or until golden brown. Cool completely. (The cookies will firm up as they cool.) Store in an airtight container. These cookies are best in taste and texture on the day they are made. Freeze for longer storage.

INGREDIENT
SPOTLIGHT

Citrus Zest

Fresh citrus zest provides incredible flavor and fragrance even in just a small amount. Adding citrus zest to cookies and baked goods serves as a clever way to incorporate fruity flavor without adding too much moisture to the dough. I like to use a handheld Microplane® grater to yield very fine zest.

Island Bliss Cookies

Naturally sweetened with honey, these cookies absolutely hit the spot if you've got a pesky sweet tooth. The trio of citrus zest along with the subtly sweet coconut and crunchy macadamia nuts unite to create a soft, chewy cookie that evokes the flavor of the tropics. Close your eyes as you take that first bite and you'll quickly be whisked away to a land of salty breezes, swaying palms, and sun-soaked beaches. Ah, bliss!

MAKES
About 18
soft and chewy cookies

SWEETNESS RATING

INGREDIENTS
1 ¾ cup unsweetened shredded coconut
½ cup raw macadamia nuts, finely chopped
⅓ cup honey
2 large eggs, lightly beaten
1 teaspoon finely grated orange zest
1 teaspoon finely grated lime zest
1 teaspoon finely grated lemon zest
¼ teaspoon sea salt

DIRECTIONS
Preheat the oven to 350°F. Line 2 baking sheets with parchment paper.

Place all of the ingredients in a large bowl and stir to combine thoroughly. Form the mixture into tightly packed balls about 1 ½-inches in diameter. Flatten each ball in your hands to about ⅓-inch thick and place on the baking sheet.

Bake for about 15 minutes until golden brown. Cool completely. Store in an airtight container.

INGREDIENT
SPOTLIGHT

Quinoa Flakes

Quinoa flakes are essentially just steamrolled quinoa. A powerhouse of nutrition, quinoa offers an array of vitamins and minerals including vitamin E and magnesium, both of which play a role in heart health. Containing all nine essential amino acids (the nutritional building blocks of protein), quinoa flakes pack nearly twice the protein of oats. They do not require cooking prior to using in baked good recipes. Just toss them into the dough as you would oats for extra texture and nutrients.

Quinoa Cranberry Orange Cookies

Slightly nutty with a chewy texture, these cookies pair well with tea and coffee. Quinoa flakes add protein and fiber while the walnuts provide a healthy dose of essential omega-3 fats.

MAKES
About 20 chewy cookies

SWEETNESS RATING

🥄🥄🥄

INGREDIENTS

2/3 cup coconut sugar

3 tablespoons unsweetened almond or rice milk

3 tablespoons Grade B maple syrup

2 tablespoons extra-virgin olive oil

1 tablespoon finely grated orange zest

1 ½ cups quinoa flakes

1 cup raw walnuts

¼ cup (29 grams) coconut flour

2 tablespoons whole psyllium husks

½ teaspoon baking soda

½ teaspoon sea salt

1/3 cup dried cranberries, preferably fruit juice-sweetened

DIRECTIONS

Preheat the oven to 350°F. Line 2 baking sheets with parchment paper.

In a large bowl, whisk together the coconut sugar, almond milk, maple syrup, olive oil, and orange zest to combine. Set aside.

In a food processor fitted with the steel blade, process the quinoa flakes, walnuts, coconut flour, psyllium husks, baking soda, and salt for 30 seconds. Stir the dry ingredients into the wet ingredients to thoroughly combine. Stir in the dried cranberries.

Roll heaping tablespoons of the dough into balls. Place the balls 2 inches apart on the lined baking sheets. Using your palm or fingertips, flatten each ball to about 1/3-inch thick.

Bake for 8–10 minutes or until lightly browned. Do not over-bake. Cool completely. Store in an airtight container.

NIBBY COCOA OATMEAL COOKIES (Page 41)

CHOCOLATE
COOKIES

Making refined sugar-free chocolate cookies is no easy task, since almost all brands of chocolate bars and chips are sweetened with refined cane sugar. But don't be discouraged, because in this section you'll find some of my favorite chocolate cookies that are entirely naturally sweetened. When I eat these cookies, I honestly don't miss the sugar one bit. I think you'll agree.

Gluten-Free Oats

It is important to seek out certified gluten-free oats as they are often harvested and processed with equipment that handles wheat, too. Oats add toothsome texture and earthy flavor to cookies. If you'd like to incorporate them into your other cookie recipes, try replacing ¼-½ cup of the flour with oats for added nutrition.

Nibby Cocoa Oatmeal Cookies

Dark chocolate-lovers, rejoice! You'll love these bittersweet cocoa cookies flecked with rolled oats and crunchy cacao nibs. Wash them down with a cold glass of almond milk for true cookie bliss.

MAKES
About 16
chewy and crunchy cookies

SWEETNESS RATING

INGREDIENTS

1 ¼ cups (120 grams) blanched almond flour
1 ¼ cups gluten-free rolled oats
¼ cup unsweetened cocoa powder
1 teaspoon ground cinnamon
½ teaspoon baking powder
¼ teaspoon sea salt
⅓ cup Grade B maple syrup
⅓ cup virgin coconut oil, melted
2 teaspoons vanilla extract
¼ cup cacao nibs *or chocolate chips*

DIRECTIONS

Preheat the oven to 350°F. Line 2 baking sheets with parchment paper.

In a large bowl, combine the almond flour, oats, cocoa powder, cinnamon, baking powder, and salt. In a small bowl, whisk together the maple syrup, coconut oil, and vanilla to combine. Stir the wet ingredients into the dry. Stir in the cacao nibs. Let the dough stand at room temperature for 5–10 minutes.

Form the dough into 1 ½-inch balls and place them 2 inches apart on the baking sheets. Flatten each ball to about ½-inch thick with your fingertips or the bottom of a glass.

Bake for 10–12 minutes until just firm to the touch. Cool completely. (The cookies will continue to firm up as they cool.). Store in an airtight container.

BAKING
STORIES

Biscotti History

Biscotti are twice-baked biscuit cookies that originated in Tuscany. It is believed that early biscotti recipes were prepared because the biscuits could withstand long periods of time in storage while retaining a crisp texture. In Italy, biscotti typically accompany sweet wine as a light dessert, but they're also commonly served with coffee and tea. Good biscotti should be just a tad crumbly with a dry texture and subtly sweet flavor, perfect for dunking.

Orange-Scented Chocolate Biscotti

The ultimate treat with a warm cup of tea, these not-too-sweet biscotti cookies are crunchy and chocolatey with just a hint of orange zest for fruity citrus flavor.

MAKES

About 14 crunchy biscotti

SWEETNESS RATING

INGREDIENTS

1 ¾ cup (168 grams) blanched almond flour

¼ cup plus 2 tablespoons unsweetened cocoa powder

⅓ cup coconut sugar

1 tablespoon whole psyllium husks

1 teaspoon baking powder

½ teaspoon sea salt

¼ cup virgin coconut oil, melted

1 large egg, room temperature

1 tablespoon Grade B maple syrup or honey

1 tablespoon finely grated orange zest

1 ounce unsweetened chocolate, finely chopped

DIRECTIONS

Preheat the oven to 350°F. Line a baking sheet with parchment paper.

In a large bowl, whisk together the almond flour, cocoa powder, coconut sugar, psyllium husks, baking powder, and salt. In a medium bowl, whisk together the coconut oil, egg, maple syrup, and orange zest. Stir the wet ingredients into the flour mixture to form a thick dough. Stir in the chopped chocolate.

Shape the dough into a flat log on the lined baking sheet about 9-inches long and 4-inches wide. Bake for about 20 minutes until firm to the touch and slightly cracked around the edges. Cool for 25–30 minutes. Reduce the oven to 250°F.

Using a sharp serrated knife, carefully cut the log on the diagonal into ⅓-½ inch thick slices. Be gentle, as the dough will still be slightly soft and crumbly at this point. Carefully place the biscotti cut side down on the lined baking sheet.

Bake for 18 minutes. Flip the biscotti and continue baking for another 18 minutes. Turn the oven off and leave the biscotti inside it for 15 minutes. Remove from the oven and cool completely. Store in an airtight container.

Bear Paw Freezer Treats

These fun chocolate freezer treats are a healthier play on my mom's classic Bear Claws, which were a family favorite growing up. Crispy rice cereal and sweet raisins pair perfectly with the sunflower seed butter and honey. The lightly sweetened clusters make a tasty afternoon snack for chocolate-lovers of any age.

MAKES
About 36 crunchy clusters

SWEETNESS RATING

TECHNIQUE TIP
If your baking sheets won't fit in the freezer or refrigerator, drop the clusters into parchment-lined baking dishes.

JAZZ IT UP
Feel free to add other nuts or seeds to your "paws" for more crunch and nutrition. (Think chopped almonds, walnuts, pecans, and pumpkin seeds.)

INGREDIENTS
4 cups crispy brown rice cereal
1 cup raisins or dried cherries
⅔ cup roasted salted sunflower seeds
½ cup sunflower seed butter (unsweetened)
3 ounces unsweetened chocolate, roughly chopped
⅓ cup honey
1 teaspoon ground cinnamon

DIRECTIONS
Line 2 rimmed baking sheets with parchment paper. In a large bowl, combine the rice cereal, raisins, and sunflower seeds.

In a small pot over very low heat, combine the sunflower seed butter, chocolate, honey, and cinnamon. Stir constantly until the chocolate is melted and the mixture is thick and smooth. Pour over the cereal mixture and stir to combine thoroughly.

Drop scant ¼-cupfuls (lightly packed) of the mixture onto the lined baking sheets. Transfer the treats to the freezer for about 20 minutes (or to the refrigerator for about 1 hour) to set up. Store the treats in an airtight container in the freezer.

Chocolate Raisin Brownie Drops

Chocolate-covered raisins and nuts are two of my favorite holiday nibbles that inspired these cookies. Tucked into holiday cookie tins or gift baskets, the treats are guaranteed to please any chocolate-lover. Dried cranberries or chopped dried apricots make an equally delicious swap for the raisins if you're looking for something a bit more upscale.

MAKES
About 16
chocolatey drop cookies

**SWEETNESS
RATING**

INGREDIENTS

3 ounces unsweetened chocolate, chopped

2 tablespoons honey or Grade B maple syrup

1 tablespoon virgin coconut oil

1 large egg, room temperature

⅓ cup coconut sugar

1 tablespoon plus 1 teaspoon (12 grams) brown rice flour

2 teaspoons (5 grams) arrowroot starch

¼ teaspoon baking powder

¼ teaspoon sea salt

⅓ cup raisins

⅓ cup raw almonds or walnuts, finely chopped

DIRECTIONS

Preheat the oven to 350°F. Line 2 baking sheets with parchment paper.

In a small pot over very low heat, combine the chocolate, honey, and coconut oil. Cook, stirring constantly, until just melted and smooth. Remove from heat and transfer to a medium heatproof bowl. Set aside to cool for 10–15 minutes.

Add the egg, coconut sugar, brown rice flour, arrowroot starch, baking powder, and salt to the chocolate mixture and stir vigorously to combine. Stir in the raisins and almonds. The dough will be shiny and oily.

Drop tablespoons of the dough 2 inches apart on the lined baking sheets. Bake for 10–12 minutes until dry to the touch. Cool completely. Store in an airtight container.

INGREDIENT SPOTLIGHT

Pumpkin Seeds

Pumpkin seeds, also called pepitas, have a chewy texture and subtle nutty flavor that makes them a great addition to baked goods and treats. Toasting the seeds enhances their many layers of flavor by drawing out their oils. The seeds also make a unique crunchy topping for salads, chili, and soup.

Spiced Chocolate Nuggets

Although not technically a cookie, I couldn't write this book without adding these nuggets to the line up. Why? Because they truly are super healthy! Packed with heart-healthy fats from the pumpkin seeds and almonds, they also deliver antioxidants from the cocoa, cinnamon, and ginger. Dates and maple syrup add sweetness, while the dried cranberries lend lively tang to keep things interesting. Look for fruit juice-sweetened cranberries in natural food stores.

MAKES

About 24
moist and chewy nuggets

SWEETNESS RATING

HOW TO TOAST SEEDS

To toast the seeds and nuts, place them in a dry skillet over medium heat. Cook, shaking the pan occasionally, until lightly browned and fragrant, 3–5 minutes.

INGREDIENTS

½ cup raw pumpkin seeds, toasted

¼ cup raw almonds, toasted

1 ounce unsweetened chocolate, chopped

1 tablespoon unsweetened cocoa powder

1 teaspoon ground cinnamon

½ teaspoon ground ginger

¼ teaspoon sea salt

½ cup (packed) pitted Medjool dates

¼ cup dried cranberries, preferably fruit juice-sweetened

2 tablespoons Grade B maple syrup

DIRECTIONS

In a food processor fitted with the steel blade, process the pumpkin seeds, almonds, chocolate, cocoa powder, cinnamon, ginger, and salt until finely ground, about 30 seconds. Add the dates and cranberries. Process until finely chopped, about 15 seconds. Add the maple syrup and process until the mixture forms a rough dough.

Divide the dough into 4 equal pieces. Roll each piece of dough into a log about 6- to 7-inches long. Cut each log into 6 pieces. Refrigerate the "nuggets" in an airtight container between pieces of parchment paper.

Peppermint

Natural peppermint flavoring makes a tasty addition to many culinary creations. Here are a few of my favorite ways to use it:

Add a splash to smoothies and top with raw cacao nibs for a delicious "mint chip" beverage.

Add it to chocolate cake or to your brownie batter for mouthwatering mint flavor.

Use the chocolate coating to coat banana slices, then freeze until firm.

Chocolate Covered Mint Patties

If you love the refreshing combination of chocolate and mint, you will fall head over heels in love with these treats. On the day that I developed the recipe, I literally did a fist pump in the middle of the kitchen as I took my first bite. They were just what I was looking to create: soft, moist patties coated in luxuriously rich chocolate.

MAKES
About 18
chewy patties

SWEETNESS RATING

INGREDIENTS

For the patties:
1 cup raw walnuts
3 tablespoons unsweetened cocoa powder
½ cup (packed) pitted Medjool dates
2 tablespoons virgin coconut oil, room temperature (not melted)
¼ teaspoon sea salt

For the chocolate coating:
3 ounces unsweetened chocolate, chopped
3 tablespoons Grade B maple syrup
3 tablespoons virgin coconut oil
¾ teaspoon natural peppermint flavoring

DIRECTIONS
Make the patties: In a food processor fitted with the steel blade, process the walnuts and cocoa powder until the nuts are finely ground, about 30 seconds. Add the dates, coconut oil, and salt. Process until the mixture forms a rough dough, 10–15 seconds.

Form the mixture into small patties about ¼-inch thick, using 2 teaspoons of dough per patty. Handle the patties as little as possible to avoid melting the coconut oil. Place the patties on a parchment-lined baking sheet or freezer-safe plate. Freeze for 25–30 minutes.

Make the chocolate coating: Combine the chocolate, maple syrup, and coconut oil in a small pot over very low heat. Whisk constantly until melted and smooth. Remove from heat and whisk in the peppermint flavoring.

Working quickly, dip the frozen patties in the melted cocoa mixture to coat. Return the patties to the lined baking sheet or plate and freeze until set, about 20 minutes. Store the patties in an airtight container in the freezer.

The No-Bake Solution

No-bake drop cookies are a busy mom's best friend. Growing up, my mom used to stash a batch of no-bakes every other week or so in our freezer for a quick treat to grab on the go. They're perfect when you want the comfort of a cookie without the hassle of firing up the oven for a big baking project. My mom's logic was simple and effective: serve healthy treats every once in a while and little ones will be less likely to crave store-bought junk food. See page 119 for more no-bake treat ideas.

Chocolate Hazelnut Oatmeal Drops

No-bake treats like these are proof that sometimes the simplest recipes are the tastiest. Easy to make but full of flavor and texture from the oats, they're guaranteed to satisfy just about any sweet tooth. Throw in some chocolate hazelnut spread for good measure and you've got a simple dessert that's out-of-the-park delicious.

MAKES
About 28
chewy drop clusters

SWEETNESS RATING

HOW TO TOAST HAZELNUTS
Preheat oven to 350°F. Place the hazelnuts on a rimmed baking sheet. Roast for 10–12 minutes. When the hazelnuts are cool enough to handle, rub them with a paper towel to remove the skins as best as you can. (Not all of the skins will come off. That's okay. Just try to remove most of them.)

INGREDIENTS
¼ cup coconut sugar
¼ cup virgin coconut oil
¼ cup canned coconut milk (full fat)
2 tablespoons unsweetened cocoa powder
2 tablespoons Grade B maple syrup
⅓ cup Dreamy Chocolate Hazelnut Spread (page 54)
Pinch of sea salt
2 cups gluten-free rolled oats
½ cup toasted hazelnuts, chopped
¼ cup unsweetened shredded coconut

DIRECTIONS
Line 2 baking sheets or large pans with parchment paper.

In a small pot over medium-low heat, whisk together the coconut sugar, coconut oil, coconut milk, cocoa powder, and maple syrup. Bring to a rapid simmer, whisking occasionally. Whisk in the hazelnut spread and salt. Remove from heat.

In a large bowl, combine the oats, chopped hazelnuts, and shredded coconut. Add the chocolate sauce and stir to combine thoroughly.

Drop heaping tablespoons of the mixture onto the lined baking sheets. Refrigerate or freeze until firmly set. Store in an airtight container in the refrigerator.

INGREDIENT
SPOTLIGHT

Crazy for Coconut

Because it's already naturally sweet, coconut lends itself perfectly to cookies and confections. But don't stop there! Unsweetened shredded coconut, raw or lightly toasted, adds a tropical touch to many foods. Try sprinkling it over fruit bowls, hot cereal, pudding, and warm applesauce. Add a spoonful to smoothies for a dose of healthy fat and easy-going island flavor.

Cocoa-Kissed Ginger Macaroons

Everything is better with a little chocolate, including everybody's favorite coconut cookie: the classic macaroon. The treats are crispy and nutty with a chewy center. Cocoa powder adds chocolate flavor while ground ginger adds some spicy zip.

MAKES
About 16
chewy clusters

SWEETNESS RATING

CHOCOHOLIC'S TIP
Easily turn these chewy coconut delights into Double Chocolate Macaroons. Drizzle the cooled treats with the Really Easy Chocolate Drizzle on page 55.

INGREDIENTS
2 large egg whites
¼ cup honey
1 teaspoon ground ginger
½ teaspoon sea salt
1 ½ cups unsweetened shredded coconut
2 tablespoons unsweetened cocoa powder

DIRECTIONS
Preheat the oven to 350°F. Line a baking sheet with parchment paper.

In the bottom of a large bowl, whisk the egg whites vigorously until frothy, about 1 minute. Add the honey, ginger, and salt. Whisk to combine thoroughly. Add the coconut and cocoa powder. Stir to combine.

Drop the macaroons 1–2 inches apart onto the lined baking sheet, using 1 packed tablespoon of dough per macaroon. Bake for 12–14 minutes until lightly browned. Cool completely. Store in an airtight container.

Dreamy Chocolate Hazelnut Spread

A much healthier play on Nutella, this spread knocks my socks off every time I make it. I call it Dreamy Chocolate Hazelnut Spread because I've literally had dreams about living in a castle made of this stuff. Who needs a Knight in Shining Armor? I'll take a jar of this spread and a spoon any day.

MAKES
About 1 cup

SWEETNESS RATING

INGREDIENTS

1 cup raw hazelnuts

⅓ cup canned coconut milk (full fat)

3 tablespoons Grade B maple syrup

3 tablespoons unsweetened cocoa powder

¼ teaspoon sea salt

DIRECTIONS

Preheat the oven to 350°F. Place the hazelnuts on a rimmed baking sheet. Roast for 10–12 minutes. When the hazelnuts are cool enough to handle, rub them with a paper towel to remove the skins as best as you can. (Not all of the skins will come off. That's okay. Just try to remove most of them.)

Place the hazelnuts in a food processor fitted with the steel blade. Process for about 5 minutes until a thick butter forms, stopping occasionally to scrape down the sides of the bowl with a rubber spatula.

In a small pot over medium heat, whisk together the coconut milk, maple syrup, cocoa powder, and salt. Cook just until small bubbles begin to form around the edges of the pot. Remove from heat and pour into the hazelnut butter in the food processor. Process until smooth.

Store the hazelnut spread in an airtight container in the refrigerator. Bring to room temperature before using.

Really Easy
Chocolate Drizzle

Drizzle this super simple chocolate sauce over your favorite cookies for a little extra pizazz. One batch will yield enough to drizzle at least 2 dozen cookies.

MAKES

Enough for drizzling
24+ cookies

**SWEETNESS
RATING**

**WAYS TO USE
CHOCOLATE DRIZZLE**

I'm one of the many people in this world who believe that everything tastes just a little better with chocolate. Drizzle this sauce over ice cream, fresh fruit bowls, brownies and blondies, cakes and cupcakes, muffins—anything that needs a little chocolate love. I've also stirred it into berry smoothies for a "hot fudge sundae" effect. Out of this world delicious.

INGREDIENTS

3 ounces unsweetened chocolate, chopped

3 tablespoons virgin coconut oil

3 tablespoons Grade B maple syrup or honey

DIRECTIONS

Combine all of the ingredients in a small pot over very low heat. Cook, stirring constantly, until melted and smooth. Use immediately.

CHAI SESAME SWEETIES (Page 83)

BARS
BITES & BALLS

The recipes in this section are by far some of my favorites. Little balls and bites, while small, deliver big flavor and excellent nutrition. They're easy to make and perfect for tiny helping hands. It's nearly impossible for me to pick a favorite, but I truly can't get enough of the Almond Butter Health Balls (page 79), Granola-Topped Blueberry Pie Bars (page 58) and, of course, the Bittersweet Espresso Truffle Balls (page 75) for my chocolate fix.

Granola-Topped Blueberry Pie Bars

I took one bite of these bars and my taste buds shouted, "Hello, Blueberry Pie!" The moist crust and crunchy topping of these bars paired with the juicy blueberry filling is just sublime. Don't let the rather long list of ingredients scare you. They're very easy to make.

MAKES
16
moist and fruity bars

SWEETNESS RATING

INGREDIENTS

1 cup gluten-free rolled oats

½ cup (67 grams) brown rice flour

½ cup coconut sugar

2 tablespoons whole psyllium husks

1 teaspoon ground cinnamon

½ teaspoon baking powder

½ teaspoon baking soda

¼ teaspoon sea salt

¼ cup virgin coconut oil, melted (plus extra for greasing the pan)

2 tablespoons unsweetened applesauce

1 large egg yolk

½ cup raw pecans or walnuts, finely chopped

¼ cup raisins

1 ½ cups fresh blueberries

2 tablespoons honey or Grade B maple syrup

1 tablespoon fresh lemon juice

1 tablespoon (7 grams) arrowroot starch

DIRECTIONS

Preheat the oven to 375°F. Grease an 8x8-inch baking dish with coconut oil.

In a food processor fitted with the steel blade, process the oats, brown rice flour, coconut sugar, psyllium husks, cinnamon, baking powder, baking soda, and salt for 20 seconds. Add the coconut oil, applesauce, and egg yolk. Process to combine. Using moist hands, pat half of the dough firmly and evenly into the greased baking dish. Crumble the remaining dough into a bowl and mix in the pecans and raisins. Set aside.

In a medium bowl, mix together the blueberries, honey, lemon juice, and arrowroot starch. Spoon the blueberry mixture evenly over the crust. Crumble the remaining dough over the blueberry layer and press gently to adhere.

Bake for about 25 minutes until golden brown. Cool completely at room temperature, then refrigerate for 1–2 hours before cutting into bars. Store in an airtight container in the refrigerator.

INGREDIENT
SPOTLIGHT

Berries

Always taste your berries before using them in a recipe so you can gauge their sweetness level. With super sweet berries, you can dial back on the sweetener.

If you're using berries in cake or muffin batters, toss them with a tablespoon or so of any gluten-free flour or starch before incorporating them into the dough. That little bit of flour will help "suspend" the fruit in the finished product instead of sinking to the bottom of the pan.

Lemon juice brightens the flavor of berries and helps to bring out their juices. Try tossing berries with a little fresh lemon juice before using in pies, tarts, and fruit bars.

Unless a recipe calls for frozen blueberries to be thawed, it's smart to keep frozen berries icy cold until the moment you use them. Thawed or partially thawed blueberries will streak the dough or batter with an unpleasant murky blue color.

Use Your Super Foods

There's no reason that healthy treats can't be a clever way to incorporate more super foods into your diet. Try these healthier swaps and additions in baking:

Cut back on refined sweeteners and try adding fruit purees such as applesauce and mashed bananas for a boost of natural sweetness.

Use olive oil instead of canola oil for more monounsaturated fats, which support both the cardiovascular and cognitive systems.

Instead of chocolate chips, try raw cacao nibs. They're higher in antioxidants and naturally sugar-free.

Try adding grated vegetables (such as carrots, beets, zucchini, and sweet potatoes) to cookie dough and brownie batter for extra nutrients and chewy texture.

German Chocolate Cake Bars

A cross between a cake and a brownie, these delectable bars have a chewy pecan and coconut topping that's simply mouthwatering. Unlike traditional German Chocolate Cake, these bars aren't cloyingly sweet, allowing the flavors of the dark chocolate brownie layer and the nutty topping to shine.

MAKES
16
moist and chewy bars

SWEETNESS RATING

TECHNIQUE TIP
Make sure your maple syrup and applesauce are at room temperature when you whisk them into the melted coconut oil. Cold ingredients will cause the oil to harden up.

INGREDIENTS
1 cup unsweetened almond or rice milk

¼ cup (packed) pitted Medjool dates

2 tablespoons ground chia seeds

½ cup unsweetened cocoa powder

¼ cup (24 grams) blanched almond flour

¼ cup (27 grams) arrowroot starch

½ teaspoon baking soda

¼ teaspoon baking powder

¼ teaspoon sea salt

¼ cup plus 2 tablespoons Grade B maple syrup

¼ cup virgin coconut oil, melted (plus extra for greasing the pan)

¼ cup unsweetened applesauce

1 teaspoon vanilla extract

2 large eggs, room temperature, divided use

¼ cup coconut sugar

¾ cup unsweetened shredded coconut

½ cup raw pecans or walnuts, chopped

1 ounce unsweetened chocolate, finely chopped

DIRECTIONS

Preheat the oven to 350°F. Grease an 8x8-inch baking dish with coconut oil.

In a blender, puree the almond milk with the dates until smooth. Transfer to a bowl and whisk in the ground chia seeds. Set aside.

In a large bowl, whisk together the almond flour, arrowroot starch, baking soda, baking powder, and salt. In a separate bowl, whisk together the maple syrup, coconut oil, applesauce, vanilla, and 1 egg. Pour the mixture into the dry ingredients and stir to combine. Pour the batter into the greased baking dish.

Whisk the remaining egg and coconut sugar into the almond milk mixture. Stir in the shredded coconut, pecans, and chocolate. Pour the mixture over the brownie batter in the pan, trying to spread it around as evenly as possible. Bake for 40–45 minutes until a toothpick inserted into the center of the pan comes out clean. Cool completely before cutting into 16 bars. Store in an airtight container in the refrigerator.

Pumpkin Bars with Oatmeal Pecan Crust

Autumn—with its swirling leaves, vibrant colors, and frosty evenings—is without a doubt my favorite season. And what better way to celebrate the harvest season than with a nutritious, slightly sweet pumpkin treat? These easy bars encapsulate the flavor and texture of pumpkin pie without the tedious task of preparing gluten-free pie dough. The fragrant spiced pumpkin layer and tender pecan-oat crust strike the perfect balance, beckoning you to take bite after delicious bite.

MAKES
16
bars

SWEETNESS RATING

INGREDIENT TIP

Canned or homemade pure pumpkin puree will work for this recipe. If you're using homemade puree, make sure it is very well-drained. Watery puree will make the filling too wet.

INGREDIENTS

For the crust:

Virgin coconut oil, for greasing the pan

1 cup raw pecans

1 cup gluten-free rolled oats

2 tablespoons unsweetened applesauce

1 tablespoon honey

1 teaspoon ground cinnamon

¼ teaspoon baking soda

¼ teaspoon sea salt

For the pumpkin layer:

¾ cup pumpkin puree

⅓ cup canned coconut milk (full fat)

⅓ cup honey

2 tablespoons coconut sugar

1 large egg, lightly beaten

1 teaspoon ground cinnamon

½ teaspoon ground ginger

DIRECTIONS

Preheat the oven to 400°F. Grease an 8x8-inch baking dish with coconut oil.

Make the crust: In a food processor fitted with the steel blade, process the pecans and oats until they resemble a coarse meal, about 15 seconds. Add the applesauce, honey, cinnamon, baking soda, and salt. Process until a dough just comes together, about 15 seconds. Set aside ⅓ of the mixture. Using moist hands, press the remaining ⅔ of dough into the greased pan. Bake for 12 minutes. Set aside.

Make the pumpkin layer: In a large bowl, whisk together all of the ingredients for the pumpkin layer until smooth. Pour over the warm crust. Gently tilt the pan to distribute the pumpkin mixture evenly. Place the pan in the oven and reduce the temperature to 350°F. Bake for 15 minutes.

Remove the pan from the oven and crumble the remaining dough over the top of the pumpkin layer, pressing gently to adhere. Return to the oven and bake for about 30 minutes or until deeply brown and a toothpick inserted into the center of the pan comes out clean.

Cool completely at room temperature, then refrigerate for at least 2 hours before cutting into bars. Serve chilled. Store bars in an airtight container in the refrigerator.

Pumpkin Puree

Most of the recipes I make do not use an entire can of pumpkin puree, leaving me with a scant cup or so left over. What to do, what to do?

Add a scoop of pumpkin puree to smoothies for added fiber and nutrients.

Mix puree into pancake or muffin batter. Dial back the wet ingredients by about ¼ cup for every ½ cup of puree you use.

Make a pumpkin parfait: top pumpkin puree with a drizzle of honey or maple syrup, chopped nuts, shredded coconut, and a little grated unsweetened chocolate.

Whisk the puree on the stovetop with coconut milk and spices like cumin and curry powder for a creamy pumpkin curry sauce. Serve over chicken, fish, rice, or quinoa.

WELLNESS
TIP

Get Creative with Vegetables

We're all looking to squeeze more vegetables into our busy lives, which sometimes calls for a little creativity. Here are a few tips to get you thinking outside the salad bowl:

Pack mild greens like spinach and lettuce into smoothies. It's the easiest way to add extra nutrients to your morning meal without even tasting it. Serve your smoothie with a breakfast cookie (page 23) for a sweet but nutritious start to the day!

Blend pureed vegetables (such as pumpkin or squash puree, spinach, or even cauliflower) into chocolate cake or brownie batter. The dark color of the chocolate will hide even the brightest of greens.

Added grated veggies (or fruits) to your cookies. Many of the recipes in this book, even though they don't call for veggies, can easily be enhanced with grated carrots or beets. Start with about ½ cup of grated vegetables and work your way up if the dough does not seem too moist.

Chewy Fig & Oat Bars

If you love fig newtons, then I've got just the treat for you! These no-bake bars are easy to make and taste like a moister, more flavorful version of the classic fig cookie.

MAKES
About 20
chewy bars

**SWEETNESS
RATING**
🥄🥄🥄

INGREDIENTS
1 cup dried Black Mission figs, stemmed and chopped
¾ cup plus 1 tablespoon water, divided use ~ *use less water*
1 tablespoon Grade B maple syrup or honey
1 cinnamon stick
1 ½ cups raw almonds
1 ½ cups gluten-free rolled oats
1 teaspoon ground cinnamon
½ teaspoon sea salt
½ cup (packed) pitted Medjool dates
¼ cup virgin coconut oil, melted
3 tablespoons unsweetened applesauce

DIRECTIONS

Line an 8x8-inch baking dish with parchment paper as directed on page 15.

Combine the figs, ¾ cup water, maple syrup, and cinnamon stick in a small pot over medium-high heat. Bring to a boil. Reduce the heat to a simmer, cover, and cook until the water has mostly evaporated and the figs are tender, 15–20 minutes. Remove and discard the cinnamon stick.

Transfer the fig mixture to a food processor fitted with the steel blade. Add the remaining 1 tablespoon of water and process until smooth, stopping several times to scrape down the sides of the bowl with a rubber spatula. Transfer the fig spread to a bowl and return the food processor to the stand.

Add the almonds, oats, cinnamon, and salt to the food processor. Process for 30 seconds. Add the dates and process for 15 seconds. Add the coconut oil and applesauce. Process until the mixture holds together when pinched between 2 fingers.

Reserve about 1 cup of the dough. Press the remaining dough firmly and evenly into the lined pan. Spread the fig mixture in an even layer over the dough. Crumble the reserved dough over the top of the fig layer. Press gently to adhere.

Freeze for about 1 hour or until firm. Remove the bar "slab" from the pan using the overhanging parchment paper. Cut the slab in half. Cut each half crosswise into 10 bars. Store in an airtight container in the refrigerator or freezer.

DATES, FIGS & RAISINS

Upon testing this recipe, one of my recipe testers exclaimed that these bars tasted better to her than even traditional fig newtons. It's the natural sweetness from the figs and dates that gives them their indulgent flavor. Incorporating dried fruits like these as well as raisins, dried apricots, dried currants, and prunes enhances not only the flavor and texture of baked goods, but also their nutritional profile...all while being refined sugar-free. What's not to love?

Spices

A well-stocked spice cabinet is to a home cook what a good pair of sneakers are to a marathoner. Both can take you a long way! Although cinnamon and nutmeg are the classic baking duo, branch out and get creative. Try ground ginger, cardamom, coriander, fennel seeds, and even peppercorns. Use spices as a springboard for creating your own unique flavor combinations. A few of my favorite combos:

Cardamom and maple syrup
Fennel seeds and orange zest
Pepper and sage
Nutmeg, cardamom, and apples
Ginger and lemon zest
Cinnamon, orange zest, and coconut

Blueberry Gingerbread Cookie Dough Balls

A delightful nut-free treat, these balls remind me of ginger cookie dough. Dried blueberries add an unexpected flavor, but if you can't find them feel free to swap in dried cranberries or raisins instead.

MAKES
25–30
chewy balls

SWEETNESS RATING

INGREDIENTS
1 ¾ cup raw sunflower seeds
2 teaspoons ground cinnamon
¾ teaspoon ground ginger
½ teaspoon sea salt
¾ cup (packed) pitted Medjool dates
1 tablespoon unsweetened applesauce
1 tablespoon Grade B maple syrup
½ cup dried blueberries

DIRECTIONS
Place the sunflower seeds in a large skillet set over medium heat. Toast, stirring occasionally, until golden brown and fragrant, 4–5 minutes.

Transfer the hot sunflower seeds to a food processor fitted with the steel blade. Add the cinnamon, ginger, and salt and process for 30 seconds. Add the dates and process for 20 seconds. Add the applesauce and maple syrup. Process until the dough holds together when pinched between your fingers. Add the blueberries and pulse a few times just to combine.

Roll the dough into 1–1 ½ inch balls. Store in an airtight container in the refrigerator.

HEALTHY
TIP

Frozen Assets

I created all of the recipes in this book with the freezer in mind, making sure that every single recipe would be freezer friendly. Not only does this make storing cookies a whole lot easier for those with limited space, but it is also a healthful choice. When sweets and treats aren't out on the counter tempting us to take a nibble every time we walk by, we'll be more likely to save them for special times when we want to indulge, not binge.

Peanut Butter Freezer Fudge Cups

Stop the presses! Dairy-free, refined sugar-free fudge is just five ingredients away! The best part? This indulgent treat is easily tucked away in the freezer for longterm storage. You can thank me later when you're still fitting into your skinny jeans.

MAKES
About 24
fudge bites

SWEETNESS RATING

SWAP IT
Can't do peanuts? Swap in sunflower seed butter and roasted salted sunflower seeds for peanut butter and peanuts.

INGREDIENTS
¾ cup canned coconut milk (full fat)
½ cup creamy peanut butter (unsweetened)
¼ cup honey, or more to taste
2 ounces unsweetened chocolate, roughly chopped
¼ cup roasted salted peanuts, chopped

DIRECTIONS
In a small pot, combine the coconut milk, peanut butter, ¼ cup honey, and chocolate. Cook over very low heat, stirring constantly, until melted and smooth. Taste and add more honey if desired.

Line 24 mini muffin cups with mini paper liners. Spoon the fudge into the cups and spread it out evenly. Sprinkle the peanuts over the top. Transfer to the freezer and chill until firmly set, about 1 hour.

Store the fudge cups in the freezer in an airtight container. Thaw for several minutes at room temperature before serving.

BAKING
STORIES

Truffle Tales

Long before I began creating gluten-free treats, I operated a small chocolate candy business out of my home for a few years, selling treats to family and friends around the holidays. The espresso truffles were a smash hit. It seems that everyone loves the European pairing of chocolate and coffee—even me, a non-coffee drinker through and through. Some duos are just too delicious to resist!

Bittersweet Espresso Truffle Balls

Shh...don't tell anyone that these deletable espresso truffles are made with black beans. I promise they'll never know. Even non-coffee drinkers (like me) will love their intensely chocolatey flavor and smooth texture.

MAKES

About 24
bittersweet truffles

SWEETNESS RATING

INGREDIENTS

For the truffles:

1 cup cooked black beans

3 tablespoons unsweetened cocoa powder

3 tablespoons Grade B maple syrup

2 tablespoons virgin coconut oil, room temperature (not melted)

1 tablespoon finely ground espresso beans

2 tablespoons (15 grams) coconut flour

For the chocolate coating:

2 ounces unsweetened chocolate

2 tablespoons virgin coconut oil

2 tablespoons Grade B maple syrup or honey, plus more to taste

DIRECTIONS

Make the truffles: In a food processor fitted with the steel blade, process the black beans, cocoa powder, maple syrup, coconut oil, and ground espresso beans until thick and creamy, about 2 minutes. Sift the coconut flour over the mixture. Process until thoroughly incorporated, about 30 seconds.

Roll the dough into 1-inch balls. Place the balls on a parchment-lined plate or baking sheet. Freeze for 20–30 minutes.

Make the chocolate coating: In a small pot over very low heat, combine the chocolate, coconut oil, and maple syrup. Cook, stirring constantly, until melted and smooth. Remove from heat. Taste and add more maple syrup for extra sweetness if desired.

Dip the frozen truffle balls in the chocolate mixture to coat. Return the balls to the plate or baking sheet and freeze until the chocolate is set, about 15 minutes. Store the balls in an airtight container in the refrigerator.

Sunflower Brownie Freezer Treats

Sometimes I want a bite of something rich and chocolatey to curb a sweet tooth, but I don't need an entire chocolate cake or pan of brownies tempting me from the kitchen. So I keep a few of these treats stashed in the freezer to serve as the perfect way to healthfully combat my cocoa cravings without sacrificing good nutrition.

MAKES
About 18
chewy balls

SWEETNESS RATING

JAZZ IT UP
Feel free to roll your balls in chopped nuts or shredded coconut for added texture and eye appeal.

INGREDIENTS
¼ cup plus 2 tablespoons raw sunflower seeds, divided use
½ cup sunflower seed butter (unsweetened)
3 tablespoons unsweetened applesauce
¼ cup coconut sugar
2 tablespoons virgin coconut oil, melted
⅓ cup quinoa flakes
2 tablespoons (15 grams) coconut flour
2 tablespoons unsweetened cocoa powder
2 tablespoons raisins or dried currants

DIRECTIONS
In a coffee grinder or small food processor, grind ¼ cup of the sunflower seeds to form a meal. Set aside.

In a large bowl with an electric mixer, beat together the sunflower seed butter, applesauce, coconut sugar, and coconut oil to combine. Add the reserved sunflower seed meal, quinoa flakes, coconut flour, and cocoa powder. Beat to combine. Stir in the raisins and remaining 2 tablespoons sunflower seeds.

Form the dough into 1–1 ½-inch balls. Place the balls onto a parchment-lined plate or baking dish and freeze until firm, about 1 hour. Transfer the balls to an airtight container and store in the freezer until ready to serve. Thaw for 3–5 minutes before serving.

Cookie Dough Squares

Okay, I'll admit it. Sometimes I make cookies just so I can eat the dough. That's why I created this recipe. It's designed to be eaten straight from the refrigerator, no baking required. The squares are a cute variation on traditional balls of cookie dough, but you can certainly roll the dough into balls instead if you prefer. Late night cookie dough cravings be gone!

MAKES
Varies depending on the size you cut your squares

SWEETNESS RATING

INGREDIENTS

⅓ cup unsweetened applesauce

¼ cup honey or Grade B maple syrup

3 tablespoons virgin coconut oil, melted

2 tablespoons ground chia seeds

1 teaspoon vanilla extract

¼ teaspoon sea salt

1 cup (96 grams) blanched almond flour

⅓ cup (39 grams) coconut flour

2 tablespoons coconut sugar

1 ounce unsweetened chocolate, finely chopped

DIRECTIONS

Line an 8x8-inch baking dish with parchment paper as directed on page 15.

In a large bowl, combine the applesauce, honey, coconut oil, ground chia seeds, vanilla, and salt. Stir well. Add the almond flour, coconut flour, and coconut sugar. Stir to form a thick dough. Stir in the chopped chocolate. Let the dough rest for 5 minutes.

Press the dough evenly into the lined baking dish. Freeze for 1 hour or until firm. Remove the "slab" of dough from the pan using the overhanging parchment paper. Cut it into small squares of desired size. Store in an airtight container in the refrigerator.

HEALING
BITES

The Little Nibbles

After initially going gluten-free, I had to regain about 20 pounds of weight that I'd lost due to my food allergies. This was no easy task. I found that my best trick was eating frequently in small amounts, incorporating plenty of snacks. Balls like these were my go-to afternoon treat. Easy to digest and not too heavy or dense, they set well with my sensitive stomach and tasted good to me at a time when not much else did. It's often the little nibbles that are most nourishing to our bodies during times of immune suppression and stress.

Almond Butter Health Balls

If a person could buy stock in almond butter, I'd say sign me up! It's my go-to dip for apples, celery and carrot sticks, crackers, and more. One of my favorite ways to enjoy creamy raw almond butter is in these chewy and gooey snack balls. Packed with plant-based protein and healthy fats, just one will really stick with you. But heads up: they can be very addicting, especially for almond lovers like me. You've been warned!

MAKES
About 24
rich and gooey balls

SWEETNESS RATING

INGREDIENTS
1 cup creamy raw almond butter (unsweetened)
Scant ⅓ cup honey
1 tablespoon unsweetened cocoa powder
1 teaspoon ground cinnamon
¼ teaspoon sea salt
½ cup unsweetened shredded coconut
⅓ cup (packed) pitted Medjool dates, chopped
¼ cup raw sunflower seeds
⅓ – ½ cup raw sesame seeds, for rolling

DIRECTIONS
In a large bowl, mix together the almond butter, honey, cocoa powder, cinnamon, and salt to combine. Stir in the shredded coconut, dates, and sunflower seeds.

Form the dough into 1 ½-inch balls, handling them as little as possible to avoid melting the almond butter too much. Roll the balls in the sesame seeds to coat. Store in an airtight container in the refrigerator. (The balls taste best after they have had a chance to firm up in the refrigerator for several hours.)

Apple Carrot Quinoa Balls

These nut-free treats are sweet and chewy but secretly nutritious! Carrots, apples, ground chia seeds, and quinoa flakes add fiber and vitamins. Sunflower seed butter acts as the binder for the balls, keeping them together in good shape while they bake. Perfect for little hands, put these balls out for an after school snack and watch them disappear.

MAKES

About 18
moist and chewy balls

**SWEETNESS
RATING**

INGREDIENTS

1 cup (loosely packed) coarsely grated carrots
    (about 2 medium carrots, grated)
½ cup (packed) coarsely grated peeled apple,
    such as Gala or Fuji (about 1 medium apple, grated)
½ cup quinoa flakes
⅓ cup creamy sunflower seed butter (unsweetened)
2 tablespoons Grade B maple syrup
1 tablespoon ground chia seeds
1 teaspoon ground cinnamon
¼ teaspoon baking soda
¼ teaspoon sea salt
¼ cup raisins or dried currants

DIRECTIONS

Preheat the oven to 350°F. Line a baking sheet with parchment paper.

In a large bowl, combine all of the ingredients except the raisins. Stir to combine thoroughly and form a cohesive mass of dough. Stir in the raisins.

Using moist hands, roll tablespoons of the dough into balls and place them 1–2 inches apart on the lined baking sheet. Bake the balls for about 20 minutes. Cool completely. Store in an airtight container in the refrigerator.

Figgy Cinnamon
Snack Balls

As a special treat when I was young, my mom used to slather warm English muffins with butter, cinnamon, and sugar for me for breakfast. On mornings when I find myself craving Mom's decadent buttery toast, I reach for these spiced snack balls. They're bound together with a paste of dried Black Mission figs that sneakily packs in fiber and antioxidants, too.

MAKES
About 15
crunchy and chewy balls

**SWEETNESS
RATING**

INGREDIENTS
2 cups gluten-free crisp brown rice cereal
¼ cup raw sunflower seeds
2 teaspoons ground cinnamon
½ teaspoon ground ginger
¼ teaspoon sea salt
⅔ cup dried Black Mission figs, stemmed and roughly chopped
3 tablespoons unsweetened applesauce
1 tablespoon Grade B maple syrup
1 large egg white

DIRECTIONS
Preheat the oven to 350°F. Line a baking sheet with parchment paper.

In a food processor fitted with the steel blade, process the rice cereal, sunflower seeds, cinnamon, ginger, and salt until finely ground, about 30 seconds. Transfer to a large bowl and return the food processor to the stand.

Place the figs, applesauce, and maple syrup in the food processor. Process until the figs are very finely chopped and beginning to form a paste, about 2 minutes, stopping often to scrape down the sides of the bowl with a rubber spatula. Add the fig paste to the bowl with the rice cereal mixture. Knead with your hands to combine. Stir in the egg white.

Form the dough into small balls about 1 ½-inches in diameter. Place them 1–2 inches apart on the lined baking sheet.

Bake for about 15 minutes until deeply browned and firm to the touch. Cool completely. Store in an airtight container.

INGREDIENT
SPOTLIGHT

Tahini

Densely nutritious, tahini (sesame seed butter) is rich in calcium, magnesium, copper, and zinc. Use it to replace some of the oil in baked goods such as muffins and quick breads. In savory cooking, it makes a wonderful sauce for chicken and vegetables when whisked with coconut milk and lemon juice.

Chai Sesame Sweeties

Who would've thought that the pairing of robust, earthy sesame tahini with warm and toasty chai spices could be so uniquely delicious? These treats bring ethnic Middle-Eastern flavor right into the heart of your kitchen. If you don't care for the flavor of tahini, try another nut butter instead.

MAKES

About 16 moist balls

SWEETNESS RATING

TECHNIQUE TIP

To toast the cashews, place them in a dry skillet set over medium heat. Toast, shaking the pan occasionally, until fragrant and lightly golden, 4–5 minutes.

INGREDIENTS

⅔ cup raw cashews, toasted

⅓ cup sesame tahini

1 teaspoon ground cinnamon

½ teaspoon ground cardamom

¼ teaspoon freshly grated nutmeg

¼ teaspoon sea salt

¼ cup Grade B maple syrup

DIRECTIONS

In a food processor fitted with the steel blade, grind the cashews to form a coarse flour, about 25 seconds. Add the tahini, cinnamon, cardamom, nutmeg, and salt. Process to combine. Add the maple syrup and process just until the mixture forms a ball.

Roll the dough into 1-inch balls. (Don't worry if the dough is oily. That will disappear as the balls chill.) Refrigerate for at least 1 hour before serving. Store in an airtight container in the refrigerator.

ALMOND & PECAN COOKIES (Page 94)

SPECIAL
OCCASION COOKIES

Some of the recipes in this section are a bit more tedious in terms of preparation than others in this book, deeming them worthy of special celebrations. The Almond & Pecan Cookies (page 94) and Pistachio Chocolate Twists (page 95) are two of my favorites to serve around the holidays. The Grown-Up Monster Cookies (page 91) are indulgent enough to serve as a casual dessert for birthdays and other parties. Full of elegance and charm, these treats are sure to delight cookie-lovers of any age.

Coffee Cake Cookies

Moist and buttery, these treats taste like cinnamon coffee cake in cookie form. The pecan streusel is the ultimate sweet and crunchy topping for the soft cookies.

MAKES
About 22
moist and tender cookies

SWEETNESS RATING

INGREDIENTS

For the streusel:
⅓ cup raw pecans, finely chopped
3 tablespoons coconut sugar
1 tablespoon virgin coconut oil, room temperature (not melted)
1 tablespoon unsweetened applesauce
2 teaspoons ground cinnamon

For the cookies:
½ cup (packed) pitted Medjool dates
¼ cup unsweetened applesauce
¼ cup plus 2 tablespoons honey or Grade B maple syrup
3 tablespoons virgin coconut oil, room temperature (not melted)
3 tablespoons ground flaxseed
¾ cup creamy raw almond butter (unsweetened)
1 cup quinoa flakes
⅓ cup (45 grams) brown rice flour
1 teaspoon baking soda
½ teaspoon sea salt

DIRECTIONS

Preheat the oven to 350°F. Line 2 baking sheets with parchment paper.

Make the streusel: Using your fingertips, combine all of the streusel ingredients in a small bowl to form a moist and crumbly mixture. Set aside.

Make the cookies: Cover the dates with hot water and soak for about 10 minutes. Drain well and add to the bowl of a food processor fitted with the steel blade. Add the applesauce, honey, coconut oil, and flaxseed. Puree until smooth. Transfer to a large mixing bowl.

Stir in the almond butter until thoroughly combined. Add the quinoa flakes, brown rice flour, baking soda, and salt. Stir to form a thick and sticky dough. Drop heaping tablespoons of the dough 2 inches apart on the lined baking sheets. Using moist fingertips, flatten each cookie to about 1/3 -inch thick.

Sprinkle a little bit of the pecan streusel on top of each cookie, pressing gently to adhere. Bake the cookies for about 15 minutes until deeply golden brown. Cool completely. Store in an airtight container.

PECAN PERFECTION

Of all the nuts, I find pecans to contain the most buttery undertones in terms of flavor. For this reason, they add a mouthwatering butter-like quality to cookies and baked goods even when used in small amounts. As with all nuts and seeds, keep pecans in the refrigerator or freezer for longterm storage.

Hawaiian Inspiration

I fell in love with the pairing of coconut and lime in no place else but sunny Hawaii. It was in February on a family vacation. We visited a local farmers' market whenever we could to stock up on the island's local macadamia nuts, coconuts, and fresh citrus. I found myself craving that delectable coconut lime duo long after we returned, so I started using it in everything from smoothies to vinaigrettes. Of course, I couldn't help but use the island inspiration for these dainty cookies, too. They're equally delicious with orange zest instead of the lime.

Coconut Lime Wafers

These delicate coconut wafers melt in your mouth like buttery shortbread the minute you take a bite. They make a light and fun dessert for luncheons, baby showers, and spring celebrations or a crunchy accompaniment to a bowl of ice cream or fresh berries.

MAKES
About 24
thin wafers

SWEETNESS RATING

INGREDIENTS

⅓ cup (45 grams) brown rice flour

⅓ cup (36 grams) arrowroot starch

⅓ cup unsweetened finely shredded coconut

¼ cup coconut sugar

1 tablespoon ground flaxseed

1 tablespoon finely grated lime zest

½ teaspoon sea salt

3 tablespoons virgin coconut oil, room temperature (not melted)

2 tablespoons canned coconut milk (full fat)

DIRECTIONS

Preheat the oven to 325°F. Line 2 baking sheets with parchment paper.

In a food processor fitted with the steel blade, process the brown rice flour, arrowroot starch, shredded coconut, coconut sugar, flaxseed, lime zest, and salt for 30 seconds. Add the coconut oil and pulse until the mixture resembles coarse meal, 10–12 one-second pulses. With the machine running, pour in the coconut milk and process until the dough just comes together. Do not over-process.

Roll the dough out to ⅛-inch thick between 2 pieces of parchment paper. Transfer the rolled out dough, parchment paper and all, to a baking sheet and freeze for 5 minutes. Carefully cut out cookies with a 2 ½-inch cookie cutter. Transfer the cookies with a metal spatula to the lined baking sheets, spacing 1 inch apart.

Re-roll the scraps of dough and cut out more cookies, continuing to freeze the rolled out dough for 5 minutes before cutting the cookies. When all of the cookies have been cut, freeze them on the baking sheets for 10 minutes.

Bake the cookies directly from the freezer for 12–15 minutes until golden brown. Cool completely before serving. Store in an airtight container.

INGREDIENT
SPOTLIGHT

Cacao Nibs

I use raw cacao nibs as a way to lend chocolatey flavor and crunch to cookies instead of chocolate chips, since they are typically sweetened with cane sugar. Ancient Mayans touted cacao as "Food for the Gods," and not just because of the rich and robust flavor. Raw cacao also boasts an impressive array of antioxidants and contains minerals such as magnesium and iron, yielding superfood at its finest!

Grown-Up Monster Cookies

With their refined sugar, chocolate chunks, and M & M's, there's no doubt that traditional monster cookies are guaranteed to result in a monster of a blood sugar crash! This grown-up twist on the classic treat swaps in high-protein almond and coconut flours for the wheat flour, natural unbleached coconut sugar for the white sugar, and a blend of raisins, walnuts, and cacao nibs for the chocolate and candy. Now here's a monster I can feel good about eating!

MAKES

About 12 hearty cookies

SWEETNESS RATING

INGREDIENTS

1 cup (96 grams) blanched almond flour

⅔ cup coconut sugar

¼ cup (29 grams) coconut flour

1 teaspoon ground cinnamon

½ teaspoon baking soda

¼ teaspoon sea salt

¼ cup creamy roasted almond butter (unsweetened)

¼ cup unsweetened applesauce

1 large egg

2 tablespoons virgin coconut oil, melted

⅓ cup raisins

⅓ cup raw walnuts or pecans, chopped

2 tablespoons cacao nibs

DIRECTIONS

Preheat the oven to 350°F. Line 2 baking sheets with parchment paper.

In a large bowl, whisk together the almond flour, coconut sugar, coconut flour, cinnamon, baking soda, and salt. In a medium bowl, whisk together the almond butter, applesauce, egg, and coconut oil to combine. Pour the wet ingredients into the dry and stir to combine thoroughly. Stir in the raisins, walnuts, and cacao nibs. Let the dough rest for 5–10 minutes.

Drop the dough 2 inches apart onto the lined baking sheets, using about 2 tablespoons of dough per cookie. Using moist fingertips, flatten each cookie to about ½-inch thick.

Bake for 12–15 minutes until golden brown. Cool completely. (The cookies will firm up as they cool.) Store in an airtight container.

Apple Oatmeal Pecan Cookies

I've packed everything I love about my mom's award-winning Caramel Apple Pie into these mouth-watering cookies. Moist, chewy, and cinnamon-scented, the cookies are jazzed up with a drizzle of gooey caramel sauce on top for the ultimate autumnal treat.

MAKES
20-22
moist and chewy cookies

SWEETNESS RATING

INGREDIENTS

For the cookies:

⅔ cup raw pecans, finely chopped

½ cup (67 grams) brown rice flour

½ cup gluten-free rolled oats

½ cup unsweetened shredded coconut

3 tablespoons ground flaxseed

2 teaspoons ground cinnamon

½ teaspoon baking powder

¼ teaspoon sea salt

½ cup (packed) coarsely grated peeled apple, such as Gala or Fuji (about 1 medium apple, grated)

¼ cup unsweetened applesauce

¼ cup Grade B maple syrup

2 tablespoons extra-virgin olive oil or melted coconut oil

For the caramel drizzle:

2 tablespoons virgin coconut oil

¼ cup coconut sugar

2 tablespoons Grade B maple syrup

¼ cup canned coconut milk (full fat)

¼ teaspoon sea salt

DIRECTIONS

Preheat the oven to 350°F. Line a baking sheet with parchment paper.

Make the cookies: In a large bowl, whisk together the pecans, brown rice flour, oats, coconut, flaxseed, cinnamon, baking powder, and salt to combine. In a separate bowl, whisk together the grated apple, applesauce, maple syrup, and olive oil. Stir the apple mixture into the dry ingredients until a thick dough forms.

Form heaping tablespoons of the dough into balls. Flatten each ball between your palms to form a cookie about ⅓-inch thick. Place the cookies 1 inch apart on the baking sheet. Bake for about 15 minutes until golden brown and firm to the touch. Set aside to cool.

Make the caramel drizzle: In a small pot over medium-low heat, melt the coconut oil. When melted, stir in the coconut sugar and maple syrup. Cook, stirring often, until foamy and rapidly bubbling. Add the coconut milk. Cook, stirring often, for 3–4 minutes. Remove from heat and stir in the salt. Cool for 5 minutes.

Drizzle the caramel sauce over the cookies on the baking sheet. (You may not use all of the sauce.) Freeze or refrigerate the cookies until the caramel is set. Store the cookies in an airtight container in the refrigerator between sheets of waxed paper.

LIKE MOTHER, LIKE DAUGHTER

I'm not kidding around when I talk about my mom's award-winning Caramel Apple Pie. It won a shiny blue ribbon in a harvest themed pie contest. Baking runs in my blood. Growing up, my mom was never one to follow a recipe very closely but her delicious improvisational treats still gained the accolades of many a lucky taster. I love incorporating the flavors of our old family favorites into new recipes with a healthier spin.

Almond & Pecan Cookies

Deck the halls with pecan cookies! These mouthwatering treats are a grain-free spin on my all-time favorite holiday cookie, pecan sandies. Although these cookies don't have the same sandy texture as their less healthy relatives, they still offer plenty of buttery flavor and bits of nutty crunch. Their sturdy texture holds up well to the rigors of transportation, making them the perfect treat to take along on that snowy evening sleigh ride.

MAKES
About 30
nutty and buttery cookies

SWEETNESS RATING

INGREDIENTS

2 cups (192 grams) blanched almond flour

½ cup raw pecans, finely chopped, plus about 30 pecan halves for garnish

3 tablespoons coconut sugar

½ teaspoon baking soda

½ teaspoon sea salt

1 large egg yolk

3 tablespoons Grade B maple syrup

2 tablespoons extra-virgin olive oil

1 tablespoon unsweetened applesauce

DIRECTIONS

In a large bowl, whisk together the almond flour, chopped pecans, coconut sugar, baking soda, and salt. In a small bowl, whisk together the egg yolk, maple syrup, olive oil, and applesauce. Pour the wet ingredients into the dry and stir to form a dough.

Divide the dough in half. Roll each half into a log about 6 inches long and 1 ½ – 2 inches in diameter. Wrap both logs in plastic wrap and freeze for 1–2 hours.

Preheat the oven to 350°F. Line 2 baking sheets with parchment paper. Unwrap the frozen logs of dough and slice each into ¼-inch thick rounds. Place the cookies about 2 inches apart on the lined baking sheets. Gently press a pecan half into the center of each cookie.

Bake for 12–15 minutes until golden brown and fragrant. Cool completely. Store in an airtight container.

Pistachio Chocolate Twists

Impress your guests with these fun but elegant chocolate twist cookies. When I developed these treats, I intentionally made them less sweet than traditional twist cookies so that the flavors of the pistachios and cocoa powder can really shine. They remind me of a softer, prettier take on biscotti.

MAKES
12
large cookie twists

SWEETNESS RATING

INGREDIENTS
1 ½ cups (144 grams) blanched almond flour
½ cup plus 2 tablespoons raw shelled pistachios, divided use
1 teaspoon baking soda
¼ teaspoon sea salt
¼ cup plus 1 tablespoon coconut sugar
1 large egg
1 tablespoon Grade B maple syrup
2 tablespoons unsweetened cocoa powder

DIRECTIONS
Preheat the oven to 350°F. Line a baking sheet with parchment paper.

In a food processor fitted with the steel blade, combine the almond flour, ½ cup of the pistachios, baking soda, salt, and coconut sugar. Process for 30 seconds. Transfer to a medium bowl. In a small bowl, whisk together the egg and maple syrup. Pour the egg mixture into the dry ingredients and stir to form a thick, slightly sticky dough. If the dough feels very sticky, add a tablespoon or two more almond flour.

Divide the dough in half. Into half of the dough, knead or stir in the cocoa powder to combine thoroughly. Divide the chocolate dough into quarters. Divide each quarter into 3 pieces. Divide the plain pistachio dough in the same manner.

Use your hands to carefully roll each piece of dough into a rope that is 4–5 inches long, creating 24 ropes. If necessary, dampen your hands slightly to keep the dough from sticking to them. Lay a chocolate rope and a pistachio rope side by side. Pinch the ends together and gently twist. Lay the twisted cookie on the lined baking sheet. Repeat with the remaining pieces of dough, spacing the twists 2 inches apart on the baking sheet.

Finely chop the remaining 2 tablespoons of pistachios. Sprinkle them over the twists, pressing gently to adhere. Bake for 8-10 minutes until golden brown. Cool completely. Store in an airtight container.

INGREDIENT
SPOTLIGHT

Herbs

Think herbs are just meant for salads and chicken? Think again! With their floral fragrance and citrusy undertones, herbs such as thyme, rosemary, sage, and tarragon work wonders in baking. For a unique flavor twist, try adding a tablespoon or two of chopped fresh herbs to muffins, cornbread, and spiced cakes. A little goes a long way.

Rosemary Buckwheat Freezer Coins

If you're looking for a savory-sweet cookie to serve as part of an appetizer spread, go with these "coins." Earthy and barely sweet, they pair well with olives, fresh fruit, and artisanal deli meats. The cookies hold up well in the freezer, too, so it's easy to make them ahead for parties and special occasions.

MAKES
24
bite-sized savory cookies

SWEETNESS RATING

INGREDIENTS

1 ½ cups (144 grams) blanched almond flour

½ cup (60 grams) buckwheat flour

2 tablespoons ground flaxseed

½ teaspoon baking soda

½ teaspoon sea salt

3 tablespoons Grade B maple syrup

2 tablespoons extra-virgin olive oil

1 tablespoon unsweetened applesauce

1 tablespoon finely chopped fresh rosemary

1 large egg yolk

DIRECTIONS

In a large bowl, whisk together the almond flour, buckwheat flour, flaxseed, baking soda, and salt. In a separate bowl, whisk together the maple syrup, olive oil, applesauce, rosemary, and egg yolk. Stir the wet ingredients into the flour mixture to form a thick dough.

Divide the dough in half. Roll each half into a log about 6 inches long and 1 ½–2 inches in diameter. Wrap both logs in plastic wrap and freeze for 1–2 hours.

Preheat the oven to 350°F. Line 2 baking sheets with parchment paper. Unwrap the frozen logs of dough and slice each log into 12 rounds. Place the cookies 2 inches apart on the lined baking sheets.

Bake for about 12 minutes until firm to the touch. Cool completely. Store in an airtight container.

INGREDIENT
SPOTLIGHT

Applesauce

Applesauce is a baker's best friend. I stock unsweetened applesauce in my pantry for use in baking and savory cooking alike. Because of its high moisture content, applesauce contributes to the softness of cookies and can act as a smart replacement for part of the oil. When whisked with ground flaxseed or chia seeds, it also works well as an egg replacement. As you get comfortable baking with applesauce, branch out and try incorporating other fruit purees (such as pear and peach) into your recipes.

Spiced Apple Raisin Drops

I make these easy drop cookies in the autumn when I'm craving warm and toasty spices. The almond butter gives them a richness that can't be beat.

MAKES

About 22
moist and rich cookies

SWEETNESS RATING

INGREDIENTS

¼ cup plus 2 tablespoons (44 grams) coconut flour

2 teaspoons ground cinnamon

½ teaspoon freshly grated nutmeg

½ teaspoon baking soda

¼ teaspoon ground ginger

¼ teaspoon sea salt

½ cup creamy roasted almond butter (unsweetened)

½ cup coconut sugar

¼ cup virgin coconut oil, room temperature (not melted)

¼ cup unsweetened applesauce

1 tablespoon ground flaxseed

½ cup (packed) coarsely grated peeled apple,
    such as Gala or Fuji (about 1 medium apple, grated)

¼ cup raisins or dried currants

DIRECTIONS

Preheat the oven to 350°F. Line 2 baking sheets with parchment paper.

In a small bowl, whisk together the coconut flour, cinnamon, nutmeg, baking soda, ginger, and salt to combine. In a large bowl with an electric mixer, beat together the almond butter, coconut sugar, coconut oil, applesauce, and ground flaxseed until creamy. Add the grated apple and beat to combine. Add the flour mixture and beat to combine. Stir in the raisins by hand.

Drop tablespoons of the dough 2 inches apart onto the lined baking sheets. Use your fingertips or palm to flatten the cookies to about ⅓-inch thick. Bake for 15–18 minutes until deeply golden. Cool completely. (The cookies will firm up as they cool.) Store in an airtight container.

CHEWY CASHEW APRICOT COOKIES (Page 108)

CLASSIC
CROWD-PLEASERS

When you're looking for an all around crowd pleasing cookie that's guaranteed to reel in the praises from family, friends, neighbors, and coworkers, turn to these cookies. Packed with nutritious ingredients and big flavors, these treats have become classics in my baking repertoire. The Chewy Cashew Apricot Cookies (page 108) may very well be my favorite cookie in this book.

Cowgirl Cookies

It's difficult to pin down the origin of cowboy cookies (or in this case, cowgirl cookies). Laden with nuts, oats, and dried fruit, I like to think that they were the original power bar, giving cowboys and cowgirls the energy to go yeehaw-ing all over the Wild West. No matter how they got their start, I highly suggest you giddy-up on over to the kitchen and make them. Right now. They're that good.

MAKES
About 24
thick and chewy cookies

SWEETNESS RATING

INGREDIENTS
1 tablespoon ground flaxseed
3 tablespoons hot water
1 cup (96 grams) blanched almond flour
⅔ cup coconut sugar
¼ cup (29 grams) coconut flour
1 teaspoon ground cinnamon
½ teaspoon baking soda
¼ teaspoon sea salt
¼ cup creamy roasted almond butter (unsweetened)
¼ cup unsweetened applesauce
2 tablespoons extra-virgin olive oil or melted virgin coconut oil
⅔ cup gluten-free rolled oats
½ cup raw pecans, finely chopped
⅓ cup raisins or dried currants
⅓ cup unsweetened shredded coconut

DIRECTIONS
Preheat the oven to 350°F. Line 2 baking sheets with parchment paper.

In a small bowl, vigorously whisk together the flaxseed and hot water for 30 seconds. Set aside.

In a large bowl, whisk together the almond flour, coconut sugar, coconut flour, cinnamon, baking soda, and salt. In a medium bowl, whisk together the almond butter, applesauce, olive oil, and flaxseed slurry to combine. Pour the wet ingredients into the dry and stir to combine thoroughly. Stir in the oats, pecans, raisins, and coconut.

Drop heaping tablespoons of the dough 2 inches apart onto the lined baking sheets. Using moist fingertips, flatten each cookie to about ⅓-inch thick.

Bake for about 12 minutes until golden brown. Cool completely. Store in an airtight container.

Peanut Butter, Honey & Banana Cookies

My mom makes a mean peanut butter, honey, and banana sandwich. Growing up, it was one of my favorite afternoon snacks split with my sister. That sandwich inspired these cookies. I've only added one extra element because there's only one thing that can make a sandwich like that even better. It is, of course, chocolate.

MAKES
About 24
moist and chewy cookies

SWEETNESS RATING

INGREDIENTS
½ cup creamy peanut butter (unsweetened)
½ cup honey
1 medium ripe banana, mashed well (about ⅓–½ cup mashed)
¼ cup virgin coconut oil, room temperature (not melted)
1 tablespoon ground chia seeds
1 teaspoon vanilla extract
1 cup gluten-free rolled oats
½ cup (67 grams) brown rice flour
½ cup (54 grams) arrowroot starch
1 teaspoon ground cinnamon
½ teaspoon baking powder
½ teaspoon baking soda
¼ teaspoon sea salt
1 ½ ounces unsweetened chocolate, chopped into small chunks

DIRECTIONS
Preheat the oven to 350°F. Line 2 baking sheets with parchment paper.

In a large bowl with an electric mixer, beat together the peanut butter, honey, mashed banana, coconut oil, ground chia seeds, and vanilla to combine. In a medium bowl, whisk together the oats, brown rice flour, arrowroot starch, cinnamon, baking powder, baking soda, and salt. Add the flour mixture to the peanut butter mixture and beat to combine. Stir in the chopped chocolate by hand.

Drop heaping tablespoons of the dough 2 inches apart onto the lined baking sheets. Bake for 12–14 minutes until lightly browned. Cool completely. Store in an airtight container.

INGREDIENT
SPOTLIGHT

Molasses

Marvelous molasses! Chock-full of healthful properties, unsulphured blackstrap molasses contains all of the nutrients that are stripped out of cane sugar when it's refined. The thick and viscous syrup packs a punch with a significant amount of iron, calcium, and copper in every tablespoon. Beyond baking, molasses adds rich flavor to chili and stew, bean and lentil dishes, and tomato-based sauces.

Buckwheat Gingerbread Cookies

Make these cookies in the fall or around the holidays. They fill the house with the alluring and irresistible scent of gingerbread as they bake. Pumpkin puree adds moisture and contributes to their cakey texture.

MAKES
About 24
cakey cookies

SWEETNESS RATING

INGREDIENT TIP
Canned or homemade pure pumpkin puree will work for this recipe. If you're using homemade puree, make sure it is very well-drained. Watery puree will make the cookie dough too moist.

INGREDIENTS
1 cup (120 grams) buckwheat flour
½ cup (54 grams) arrowroot starch
¼ cup ground flaxseed
2 tablespoons whole psyllium husks
2 teaspoons ground cinnamon
1 ½ teaspoons ground ginger
1 ½ teaspoons baking soda
½ teaspoon sea salt
½ cup virgin coconut oil, room temperature (not melted)
½ cup coconut sugar
⅓ cup pumpkin puree
3 tablespoons blackstrap molasses
1 large egg yolk
1 tablespoon finely grated orange zest
2 teaspoons vanilla extract
½ cup dried cranberries, preferably fruit juice-sweetened

DIRECTIONS
Preheat the oven to 350°F. Line 2 baking sheets with parchment paper.

In a medium bowl, whisk together the buckwheat flour, arrowroot starch, flaxseed, psyllium husks, cinnamon, ginger, baking soda, and salt.

With an electric mixer on medium speed, beat together the coconut oil and coconut sugar until creamy, about 1 minute. Add the pumpkin, molasses, egg yolk, orange zest, and vanilla. Beat to combine. Add half of the flour mixture and beat to combine. Then beat in the remaining flour mixture. Stir in the cranberries by hand.

Roll heaping tablespoons of the dough into balls. The dough may be soft and slightly oily, so it's okay if the balls don't hold their shape very well. Place the balls 2 inches apart on the lined baking sheets. Using your palm or fingertips, flatten the cookies slightly to about ¾-inch thick.

Bake for about 10 minutes until just firm to the touch around the edges. Cool completely. Store in an airtight container.

INGREDIENT
SPOTLIGHT

Buckwheat Flour

Contrary to what you may think, buckwheat flour contains no wheat
at all and is 100% gluten-free (just make sure you're using certified
gluten-free flour). It's one of my favorite flours because of its hearty,
grassy flavor and dark color. It pairs well with nuts, herbs such as
rosemary and thyme, pumpkin and other winter squashes, and spices
such as cinnamon, ginger, and nutmeg.

Two-Bite Baklava Cookies

I have only eaten baklava once in my life, but once was enough! All I remember is biting into an intensely sweet confection that seemed to rot my teeth on the spot. Inspired by the traditional Greek dessert, these two-bite cookies are a much healthier option that pack nutritious omega-3 fats into every bite. Not only are they simple to make, they also retain their sturdy texture even after an extended stay in the freezer.

MAKES
About 22
nutty cookies

SWEETNESS RATING

INGREDIENTS
2 cups raw walnuts
¼ cup (30 grams) buckwheat flour
3 tablespoons ground flaxseed
2 teaspoons finely grated orange zest
1 teaspoon ground cinnamon
½ teaspoon baking soda
½ teaspoon sea salt
3 tablespoons honey

DIRECTIONS
Preheat the oven to 350°F. Line 2 baking sheets with parchment paper.

In the bowl of a food processor fitted with the steel blade, process the walnuts, buckwheat flour, flaxseed, orange zest, cinnamon, baking soda, and salt until very finely ground, about 30 seconds. Add the honey and process until the mixture holds together when pinched between your fingers.

Roll the dough into 1-inch balls and place them on the baking sheets about 2 inches apart. Flatten each ball with the tines of a fork or your fingertips to about ¼-inch thick.

Bake for about 10 minutes or until the cookies are dry to the touch. Cool completely. Store in an airtight container.

Chewy Cashew Apricot Cookies

These cookies are high on my list of favorites. I find it impossible to stop at just one! Together with the maple syrup and cinnamon, the toasted cashews lend an intensely nutty, almost caramel-like quality to the dough. Dried apricots add a burst of sweet-tart flavor to balance out the richness of the nuts.

MAKES
About 18
chewy and nutty cookies

SWEETNESS RATING

TECHNIQUE TIP
If the tines of your fork stick to the cookie dough as you flatten, dip the fork in a little water and continue.

INGREDIENTS
1 ½ cups raw cashews
1 tablespoon virgin coconut oil
¼ cup Grade B maple syrup
½ teaspoon ground cinnamon
½ teaspoon baking soda
½ teaspoon sea salt
⅓ cup unsulphured dried apricots, finely chopped

DIRECTIONS
Preheat the oven to 350°F. Line 2 baking sheets with parchment paper.

Place the cashews in a large skillet set over medium heat. Toast, shaking the pan occasionally, until lightly browned and fragrant, 4–5 minutes. Transfer the hot cashews to a food processor fitted with the steel blade. Add the coconut oil and process for 2 minutes, stopping occasionally to scrape down the sides of the bowl with a rubber spatula.

Add the maple syrup, cinnamon, baking soda, and salt to the cashews. Process to form a smooth and oily dough. Transfer the dough to a bowl and knead or stir in the dried apricots. (Don't worry if the dough is very oily.)

Roll the dough into 1-inch balls and place them 2 inches apart on the lined baking sheets. Using the tines of a fork, flatten each cookie to ⅓-½ inch thick. Bake for about 10 minutes until lightly golden brown. Cool completely. Store in an airtight container.

Chocolate-Drizzled Peanut Butter Cookies

They may be small, but these cookies couldn't be more crowd pleasing. I've never met a person who doesn't love the marriage of chocolate and peanut butter. Whoever first came up with that classic combo receives my infinite gratitude! Try these cookies and I guarantee you'll be thanking them, too.

MAKES

About 22
chewy cookies

**SWEETNESS
RATING**

**NOT CRAZY
FOR COCONUT?**

If you don't like coconut, I encourage you to give these cookies a try anyway. The strong flavor of the peanut butter overshadows the shredded coconut so you don't even know it's there.

INGREDIENTS

3 tablespoons boiling water

1 tablespoon ground chia seeds

1 cup creamy peanut butter (unsweetened)

½ cup unsweetened shredded coconut

⅓ cup honey

1 teaspoon vanilla extract

1 teaspoon ground cinnamon

½ teaspoon baking soda

Pinch of sea salt

Really Easy Chocolate Drizzle (page 55)

DIRECTIONS

Preheat the oven to 350°F. Line 2 baking sheets with parchment paper.

Make the cookies: In a small bowl, vigorously whisk together the boiling water and ground chia seeds for 20 seconds. Set aside.

With an electric mixer on medium speed, beat together the peanut butter, shredded coconut, honey, vanilla, cinnamon, baking soda, and salt to combine. Add the chia seed mixture and beat to combine. Let the dough rest for 5 minutes.

Roll tablespoons of the dough into balls and place them 2 inches apart on the lined baking sheets. With the bottom of a glass, flatten each cookie to about ⅓-inch thick. Bake for about 10 minutes or until golden brown. Cool completely.

Prepare the chocolate drizzle. Drizzle the chocolate over the cookies with a spoon. (You may not use all of the chocolate.) Transfer the cookies to the refrigerator or freezer until the chocolate is set. Store in an airtight container in the refrigerator.

chai

Flax - egg sub
1 tbsp Ground flax = 1 egg
3 tbsp water-warm
-sit 10 minutes

WELLNESS
TIP

Healthy Holidays

Like all of the recipes in this book, these Ginger Walnut Cookies hold up like a pro in the freezer, so they're a great make-ahead option to keep stashed around the holidays for drop-in guests. No one will ever know that they're so healthy. Put out a plate of these with some hot tea and you'll be the hostess everyone's talking about! Try serving these other healthy treats around the holidays, too:

Dust fresh fruit with a bit of cinnamon before serving. Try apple and pear slices or fresh figs.

Spiced nuts and seeds make a delicious nibble to serve at appetizer parties, or package them up in glass mason jars and give them away to guests.

Nothing beats a bowl of warm homemade applesauce on a chilly winter's day. Serve with sprinkle of cinnamon and toasted walnuts or pumpkin seeds.

Ginger Walnut Cookies

Packed with a double dose of ginger and heart-healthy walnuts, these cookies make a festive addition to holiday cookie tins. Crunchy around the edges and chewy in the center, they burst with the robust flavors of dark molasses and warm spices. A small amount of applesauce contributes moisture and subtle fruity sweetness.

MAKES

About 24 chewy cookies

SWEETNESS RATING

INGREDIENTS

1 cup (134 grams) brown rice flour
½ cup (60 grams) buckwheat flour
¾ cup raw walnuts, divided use
1 tablespoon whole psyllium husks
1 ½ teaspoons ground cinnamon
1 ½ teaspoons ground ginger
1 ½ teaspoons baking soda
¼ teaspoon sea salt
¼ cup plus 2 tablespoons virgin coconut oil, at room temperature (not melted)
½ cup coconut sugar
¼ cup blackstrap molasses
1 large egg yolk
2 teaspoons finely grated ginger root
2 tablespoons unsweetened applesauce

DIRECTIONS

Preheat the oven to 325°F. Line 2 baking sheets with parchment paper.

In a food processor fitted with the steel blade, process the brown rice flour, buckwheat flour, ¼ cup walnuts, psyllium husks, cinnamon, ground ginger, baking soda, and salt until the nuts are finely ground. Set aside.

Using an electric mixer, beat together the coconut oil and coconut sugar on medium speed for about 2 minutes. Add the molasses, egg yolk, and grated ginger. Beat to combine. Add the flour mixture and beat to form a crumbly dough. Add the applesauce and beat until dough is soft and moist but not sticky. Chop the remaining ½ cup walnuts and stir them into the dough.

Form the dough into 1–1½-inch balls and place on the lined baking sheets 2 inches apart. Bake for 16–18 minutes. Cool completely. Store in an airtight container.

Rice Cereal

Here are five more ways to use rice cereal. Look for unsweetened or very lightly sweetened brown rice cereal to use in all kinds of delicious kitchen creations.

Toss crushed cereal with oats, honey, cinnamon, and melted coconut oil. Use as a crumble on top of fruit pies and tarts.

Stir it into muffin or quick bread batters for a little crunch.

Mix it with nuts, seeds, and dried fruit for healthy "from scratch" trail mix.

Layer rice cereal with pudding or fruit puree and nuts for a healthy parfait.

Use it in place of some of the oats in granola bar recipes for extra crunch and texture.

No-Bake Rice Treats

If you're a no-fuss baker who likes to be in and out of the kitchen in a flash, these treats are for you. You don't even have to turn on your oven to make these. Crispy and chewy, the bars are held together by a blend of creamy peanut butter and sweet, sticky honey.

MAKES
16
crispy and chewy squares

SWEETNESS RATING

SWAP IT
For a peanut-free treat, use sunflower seed butter instead. If you don't have dried apricots, swap in raisins, dried currants, or dried cranberries.

INGREDIENTS
⅓ cup creamy peanut butter (unsweetened)
¼ cup honey
2 tablespoons virgin coconut oil
2 cups crisp brown rice cereal
1 cup gluten-free rolled oats
½ cup unsulphured dried apricots, chopped
½ cup raw sunflower seeds

DIRECTIONS
Line an 8x8-inch baking dish with parchment paper as directed on page 15.

In a small pot over very low heat, combine the peanut butter, honey, and coconut oil. Cook, stirring constantly, until melted and smooth.

In a large bowl, combine the rice cereal, oats, apricots, and sunflower seeds. Add the peanut butter mixture and stir to combine thoroughly. Dump the mixture into the lined pan. Press it into the pan firmly and evenly with a rubber spatula or the back of a spoon.

Refrigerate until very firm, about 2 hours. Remove the bar "slab" from the pan using the overhang of parchment paper. Cut into 16 squares. Store the squares in the refrigerator in an airtight container.

APPENDIX

Guide to Allergy-Free Recipes

APPENDIX

NUT-FREE

It is generally accepted that coconut is a fruit, not a nut, and is therefore considered to be a nut-free food. Some of the recipes below contain coconut but are free of all other nuts. Please take care to eat according to your dietary needs.

Cookie Cravings

Suggestions for Super Healthy Swaps

Make healthier choices in all of your baking projects with these smart swaps.

SUGGESTION #1 Use virgin coconut oil in place of butter.

SUGGESTION #2 Try raw cacao nibs instead of chocolate chips.

SUGGESTION #4 Raisins, dried currants, and chopped dried apricots are healthful stand-ins for chopped candies.

SUGGESTION #5 Use coconut sugar instead of refined cane sugar. It can be swapped cup for cup.

SUGGESTION #6 Replace some of the flour in a recipe with ground nuts or seeds for added fiber and healthy fats.

SUGGESTION #7 Cut back on the oil and use applesauce to give baked goods moisture and subtle sweetness.

SUGGESTION #8 Use toasted unsweetened coconut in place of sprinkles.

SUGGESTION #9 Replace cow's milk with unsweetened almond milk or full fat coconut milk for a healthful dairy-free alternative.

Easy Add-Ins

Bump up the nutritional content of your treats by adding in healthy extras like these:

CHOPPED WALNUTS, ALMONDS, PECANS, OR SEEDS
Perks: Healthy fats, fiber, protein, buttery flavor, crunch

DRIED FRUIT
(Raisins, dried currants, chopped dried apricots, or chopped dates)
Perks: Natural sweetness, fruity flavor, moist and chewy texture

UNSWEETENED COCOA POWDER OR RAW CACAO NIBS
Perks: Naturally sugar-free chocolate flavor, antioxidants

CHOPPED OR MASHED FRUIT
(Apples or applesauce, mashed bananas, etc.)
Perks: Natural sweetness, moisture, binding power when whisked with ground chia seeds or flaxseeds

GROUND CHIA SEEDS OR FLAXSEEDS
Perks: Healthy fats, fiber, anti-inflammatory compounds, binding power

SPICES
(Cinnamon, nutmeg, ginger, cloves, cardamom, etc.)
Perks: Flavor, aroma, antioxidants, anti-inflammatory compounds

No-Bake Flavor Guide

No-bake treats are super simple to make and often don't even require a recipe. The basic framework goes like this: *dry ingredients, sweetener, flavorings*, and a *binder* ingredient (usually nut or seed butter) that will help hold everything together. With this structure in mind, you can come up with dozens of no-bakes!

As you're stirring everything up, if the mixture seems too wet or sloppy, add more dry ingredients. If it's too crumbly or loose, add more binder or sweetener. It's that easy.

Drop the mixture onto parchment-lined baking sheets (or into paper-lined muffin cups) and refrigerate or freeze until firm. Store them in the freezer in an airtight container. *Here are a few flavor ideas to get you started:*

OATMEAL RAISIN DROPS
Dry ingredients: gluten-free rolled oats, chopped walnuts or pecans, raisins
Binder: sunflower seed butter (unsweetened)
Sweetener: honey or Grade B maple syrup
Flavorings: cinnamon, sea salt

CRISPY PEANUT HONEY BALLS
Dry ingredients: crispy rice cereal, chopped roasted salted peanuts
Binder: creamy peanut butter (unsweetened)
Sweetener: honey
Flavorings: cinnamon, sea salt

ALMOND NUTMEG RICE TREATS
Dry ingredients: crispy rice cereal, chopped dried apricots or dates, sliced almonds
Binder: creamy roasted almond butter (unsweetened)
Sweetener: honey or Grade B maple syrup
Flavorings: nutmeg, sea salt

GRANOLA DROPS
Dry ingredients: gluten-free rolled oats, chopped nuts, raisins or dried cranberries
Binder: creamy roasted almond or sunflower seed butter (unsweetened)
Sweetener: honey or Grade B maple syrup
Flavorings: cinnamon, ginger, sea salt

CHOCOLATE ORANGE DROPS
Dry ingredients: crispy rice cereal
Binder: creamy roasted almond or sunflower seed butter (unsweetened) melted with chopped unsweetened chocolate
Sweetener: honey
Flavorings: finely grated orange zest, sea salt

Trouble Shooting Tips

Having some trouble? Here are a few common questions and answers.

My cookies always burn. What's going on?
Chances are your oven runs hotter than what it's telling you. Purchase an oven thermometer (available for an affordable price at most home and kitchen stores) to find out. If it runs hotter than what the built-in gauge indicates, decrease the temperature accordingly to prevent burning. If your cookies are consistently burning on the bottoms, try raising them up another rack or two from the floor of the oven.

My cookies bake unevenly. Some are darker and more cooked than others. Why?
All ovens have hot spots, which really can't be prevented. To ensure your cookies bake as evenly as possible, rotate the pan(s) with a 180° turn halfway through the cooking time. If you have multiple pans in the oven, rotate them from top to bottom as well.

What should I do if my baking pans warp in the heat of the oven?
The honest answer? Get new pans. High-quality stainless baking sheets are heavy duty and will not warp in the heat of the oven.

My cookies come out too thick, almost like biscuits. What should I do?
Many of the cookies in this book require a quick flatten with your fingertips or palm before going into the oven. Make sure you're flattening to the recommended height. If you are and the cookies still come out thick, feel free to flatten even more.

What should I do if my cookies end up crumbly?
First, make sure you are measuring your flour properly. Do not pack it into the cup, as this will result in more flour than necessary. Spoon the flour into the cup and level it off with a knife. Secondly, do not over-bake the cookies. Many of the recipes in this book will firm up as they cool, so don't feel like you need to continue baking if they are soft to the touch immediately upon removal from the oven.

A recipe calls for room temperature coconut oil that's not melted, but mine is liquid at room temperature. What should I do?
Measure out the oil in liquid form as called for in the recipe. Place it in the refrigerator or freezer for 10-15 minutes or until it has firmed up a bit. It should be soft and spreadable.

When stored at room temperature, my cookies become very soft. Why?
Different climates and altitudes affect cookies in various ways. Climates with higher humidity typically result in more moist cookies. To prevent your cookies from going too soft, store them in the refrigerator or freezer until you're ready to eat them.

RESOURCES

Ancient Harvest
Quinoa flakes
www.quinoa.net

Arrowhead Mills
Gluten-free flours
www.arrowheadmills.com

Benefit Your Life
*Blanched almond flour
and other natural products*
www.benefityourlife.com

Big Tree Farms
Coconut (palm) sugar
www.bigtreefarms.com

Bionaturae
Organic fruit spreads
www.bionaturae.com

Bob's Red Mill
Gluten-free flours
www.bobsredmill.com

**Frontier Natural
Products Co-op**
Organic spices
www.frontiercoop.com

Navitas Naturals
*Chia seeds, flaxseeds,
and coconut (palm) sugar*
www.navitasnaturals.com

Nuts.com
*Gluten-free flours, nuts,
and other natural products*
www.nuts.com

Spectrum
Organic cooking oils
www.spectrumorganics.com

Tropical Traditions
*Organic coconut oil
and other coconut products*
www.tropicaltraditions.com

Wholesome Sweeteners
Organic and fair trade sweeteners
www.wholesomesweeteners.com

GRATITUDE

I have been blessed beyond measure with so many people in my life who encourage and support me on a daily basis. First and foremost, I am grateful to God for placing these people in my path and using them as instruments of grace in my life. For everything I've done and all that I continue to do, to Him be all the glory.

To my sister, Brianna, and brother-in-law, Mike. Thanks for the phone calls, the video chats, the encouraging words, the pats on the back, the emails, the laughs, and the motivation to keep pressing on when things get a little rough. You both are committed, hard workers with the most positive outlook on life. You inspire me every day!

To my good friends Alisa, Amy, Alta, Cara, Carol, Kim, Maggie, and Ricki. You girls are some of the most classy, talented, warm, kindhearted, and genuinely wonderful people I know. I thank you so much for encouraging me to pursue my dreams. Don't ever give up on yours.

To Lexie, my brilliant book designer and blogging pal. Thank you for all of your creative insights, daily encouragements, and hard work throughout this project. It's a pleasure to call you my friend!

To the readers of Daily Bites, for making my recipes in your kitchens and sharing my approach to healthy food with your loved ones. You teach me something new everyday. Thank you!

And finally, to Mom and Dad. I'll never be able to thank you enough. The ups, the downs, the challenges, the triumphs—you're always there. So from the bottom of my heart, thank you. For everything.

ABOUT THE AUTHOR

HALLIE KLECKER authors the gluten-free food blog Daily Bites (www.DailyBitesBlog.com), where she shares her enthusiasm for cooking with whole, natural, unrefined foods. Hallie's first cookbook, *The Pure Kitchen*, includes 100 recipes for nutritious gluten- and dairy-free food with an emphasis on natural ingredients. For more about this title, visit www.InThePureKitchen.com.

After experiencing health issues for several years, Hallie eliminated gluten and dairy from her diet in 2008 and, as a result, has never felt better. Through living free of gluten and dairy and emphasizing pure, unrefined foods in her diet, Hallie has discovered that eating healthfully does not equal boring meals or a pantry stocked with hard-to-find ingredients. A former personal chef, Hallie received her Nutrition Educator Certification from Bauman College of Holistic Nutrition and Culinary Arts and her Personal Chef Certification from the Culinary Business Academy. She lives near Madison, Wisconsin.

INDEX

BAKING
NOTES

CPSIA information can be obtained at www.ICGtesting.com
Printed in the USA
LVOW03s0028020114

367625LV00013B/372/P